To all the kids who dream big and love speed, This book is dedicated to you! May each colored page be a new adventure, And may your creativity and passion for luxury cars grow with every stroke. Have fun and keep exploring the wonderful world of automobiles!

ANA SOUZA

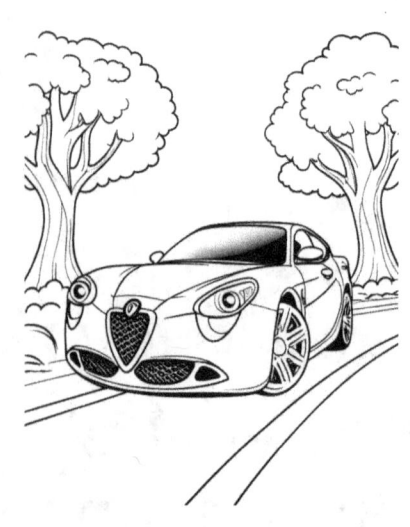
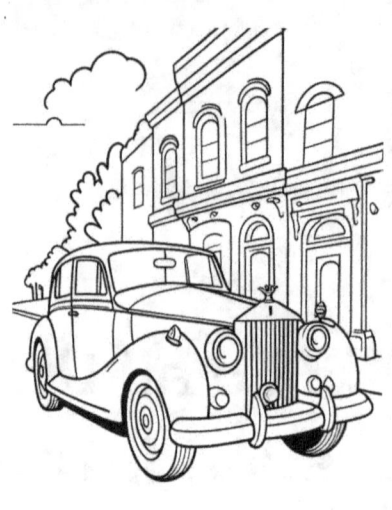

This Book Belongs To:

_____

©
A.S.P.
ANA SOUZA P.

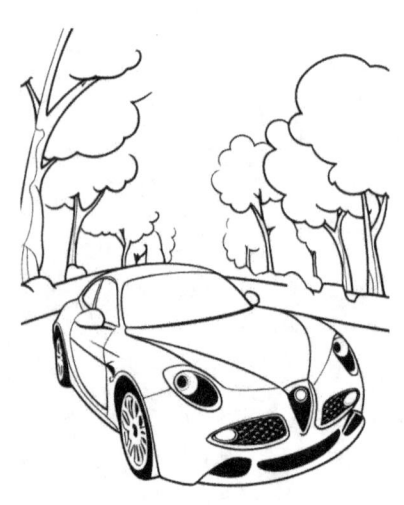
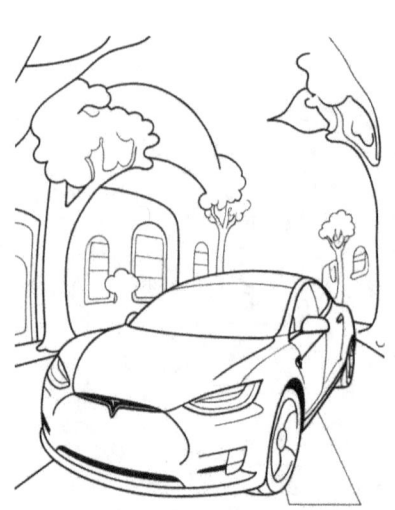

ALL RIGHTS RESERVED©
2024

No part of this publication may be reproduced, distributed, or transmitted in any form or by any means, including photocopyng recording or other electronic or mechanical methods, without the prior written permission of the publisher, except for brief quotations incorporated in critical reviews and other spedific noncommercial uses. Any unauthorized replica of this work is prohibited.

A.S.P.©
ANA SOUZA PUBLICATIONS

Test Color Page

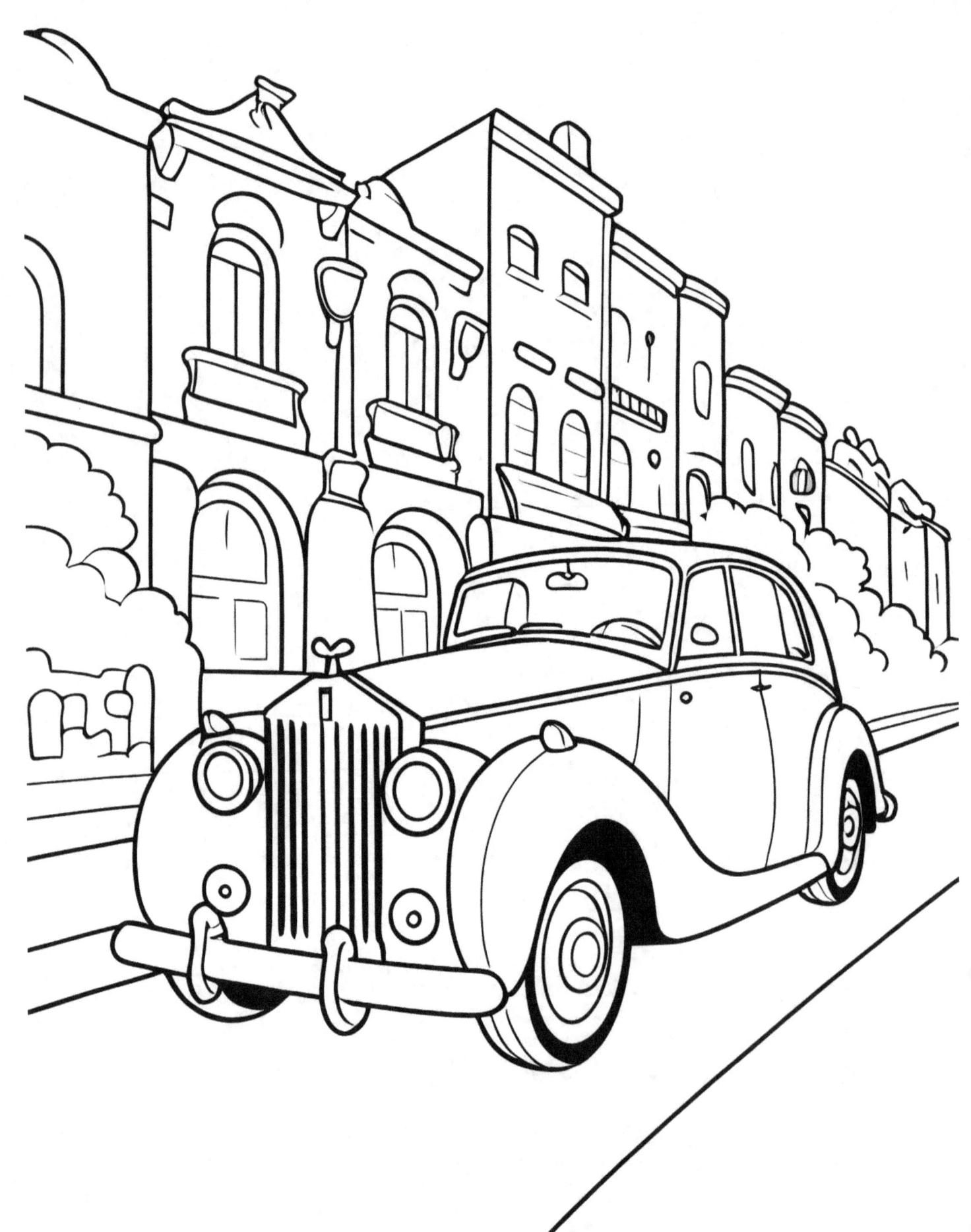

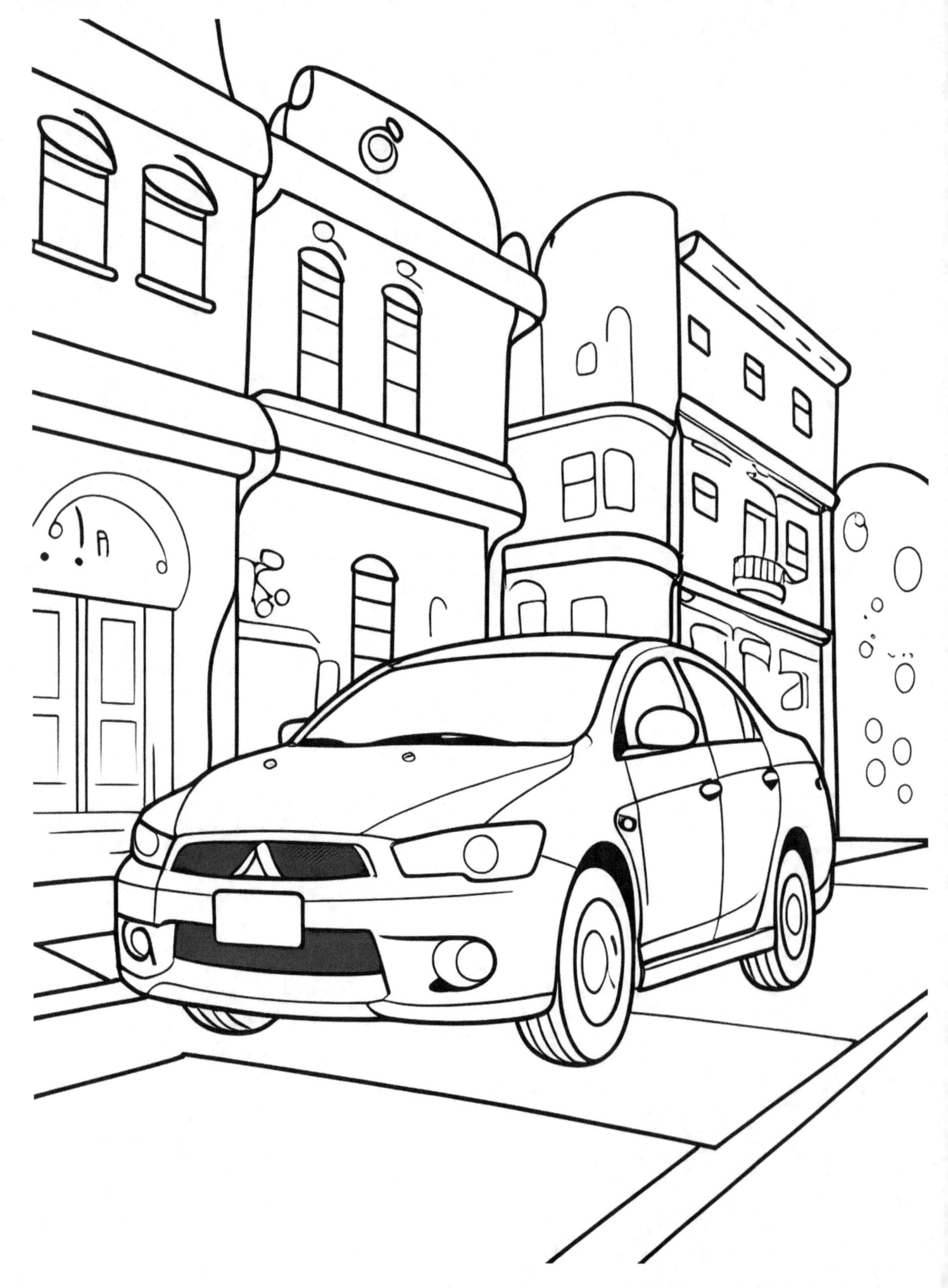

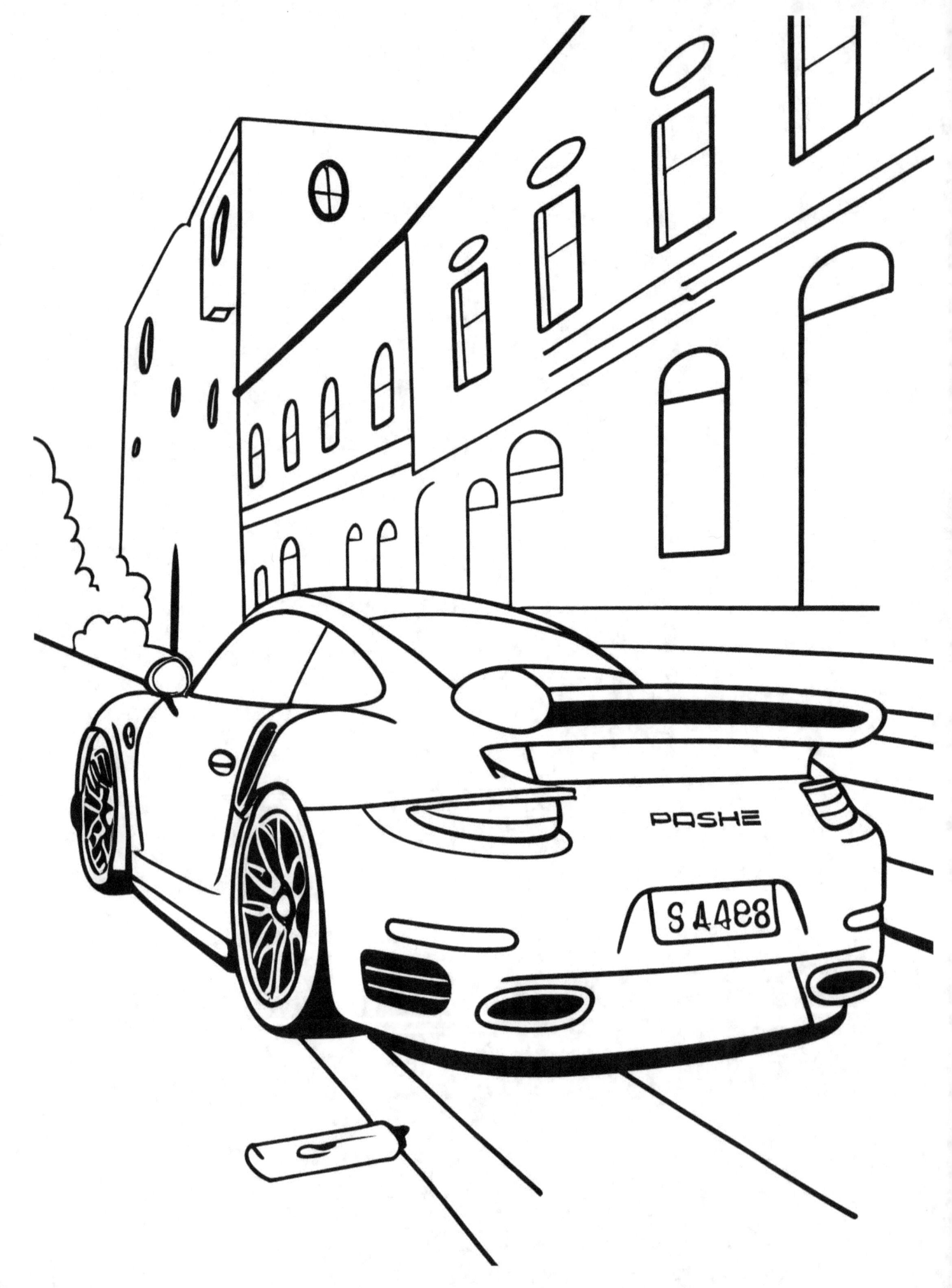

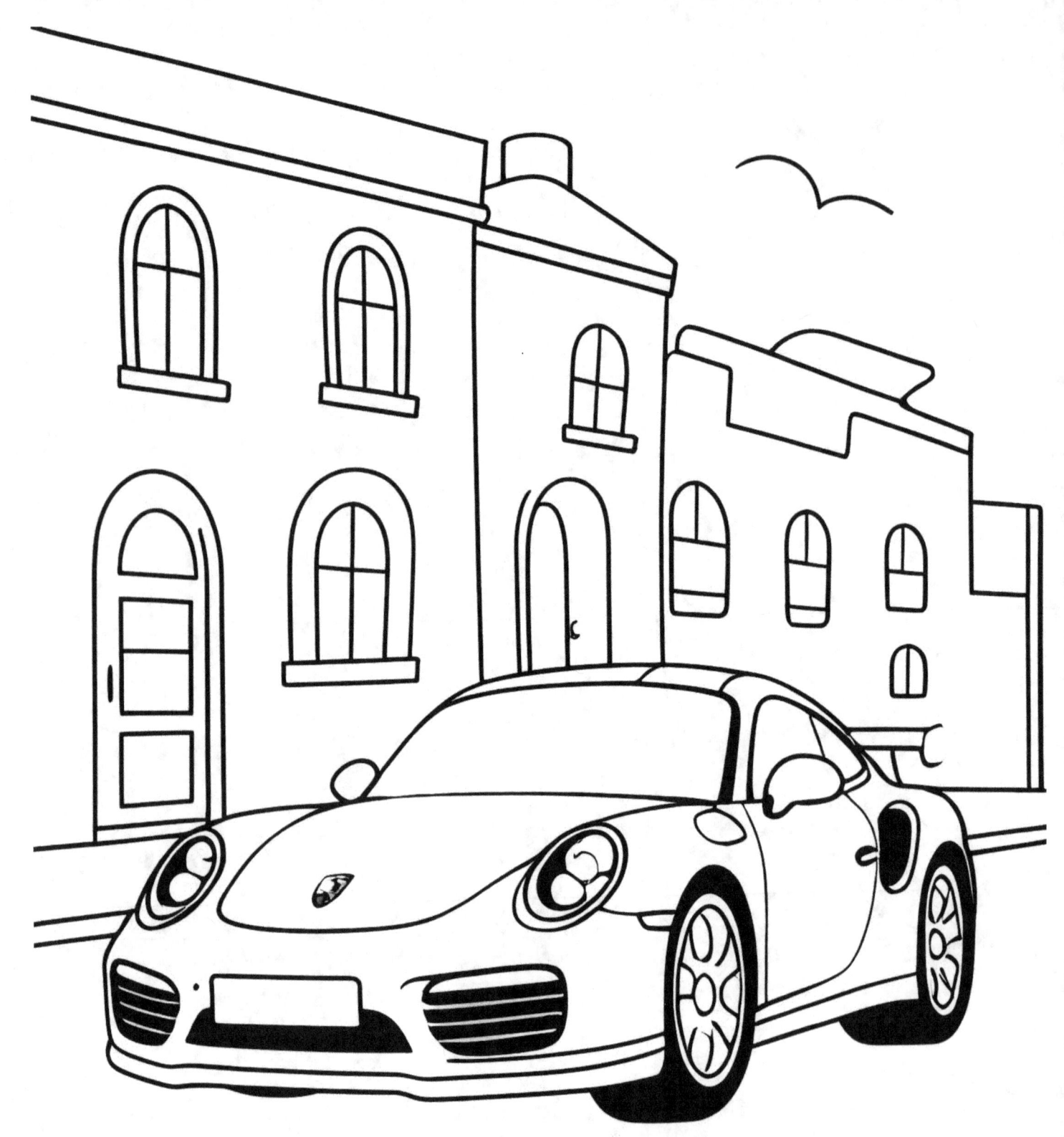

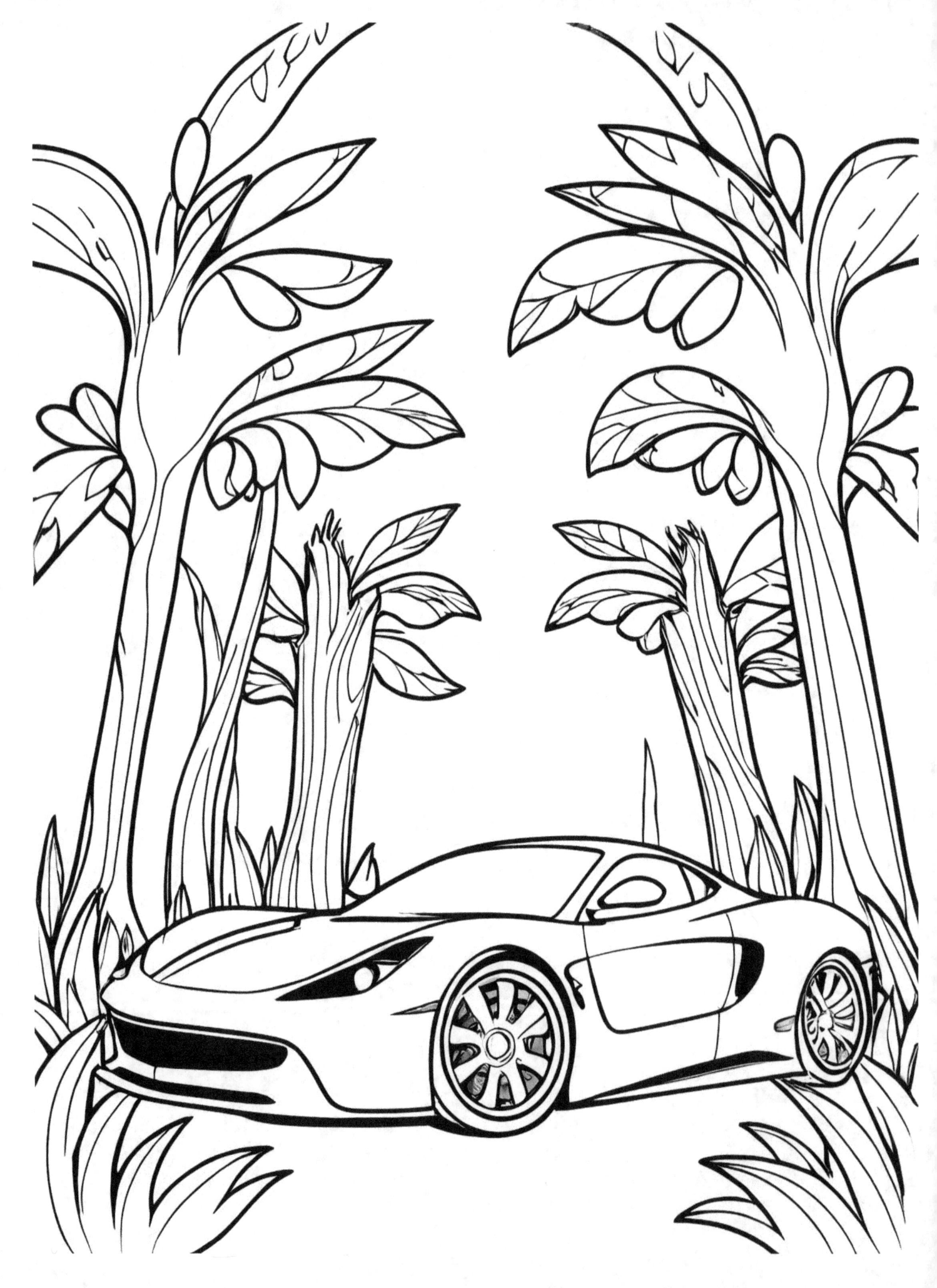

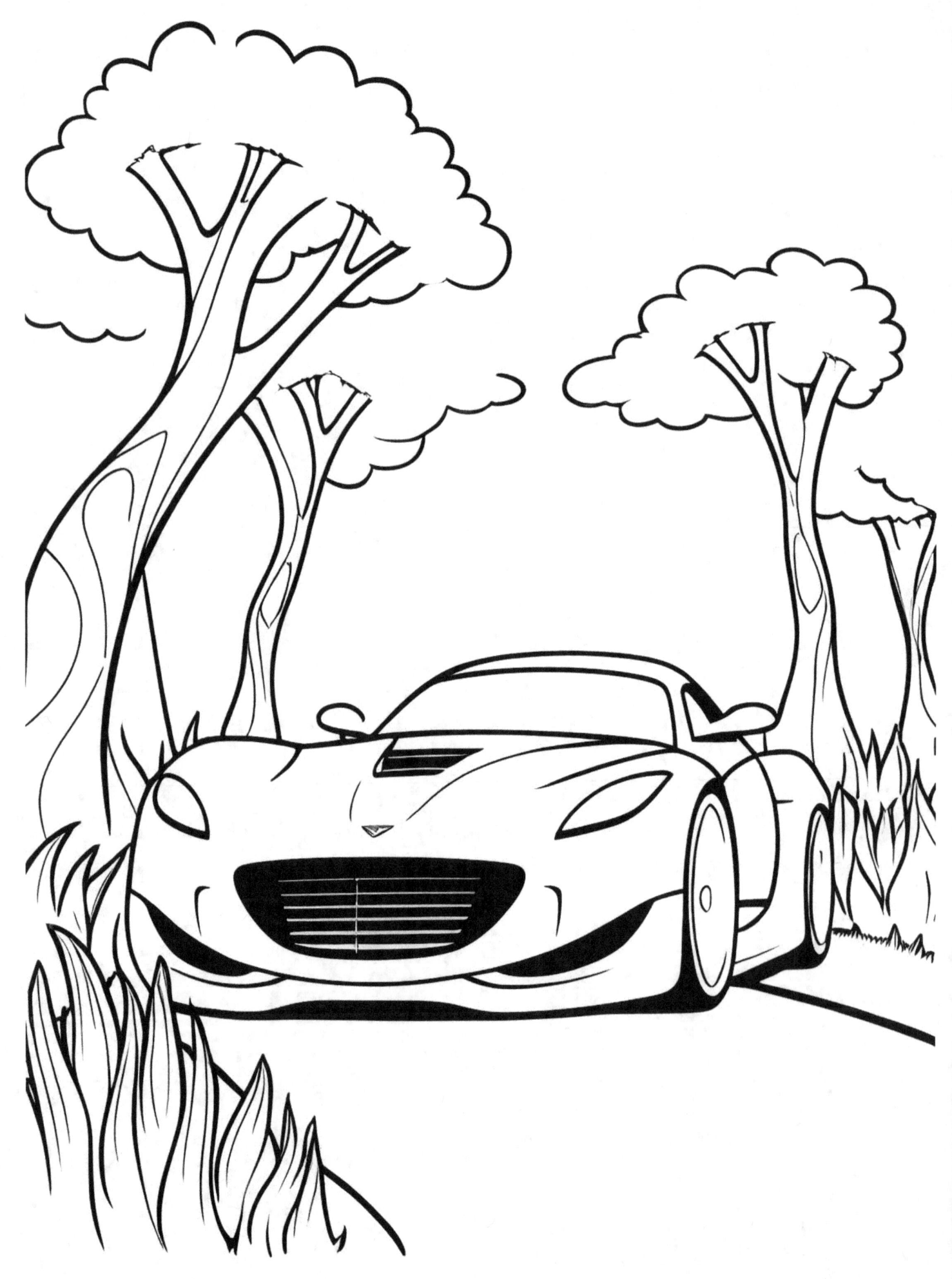

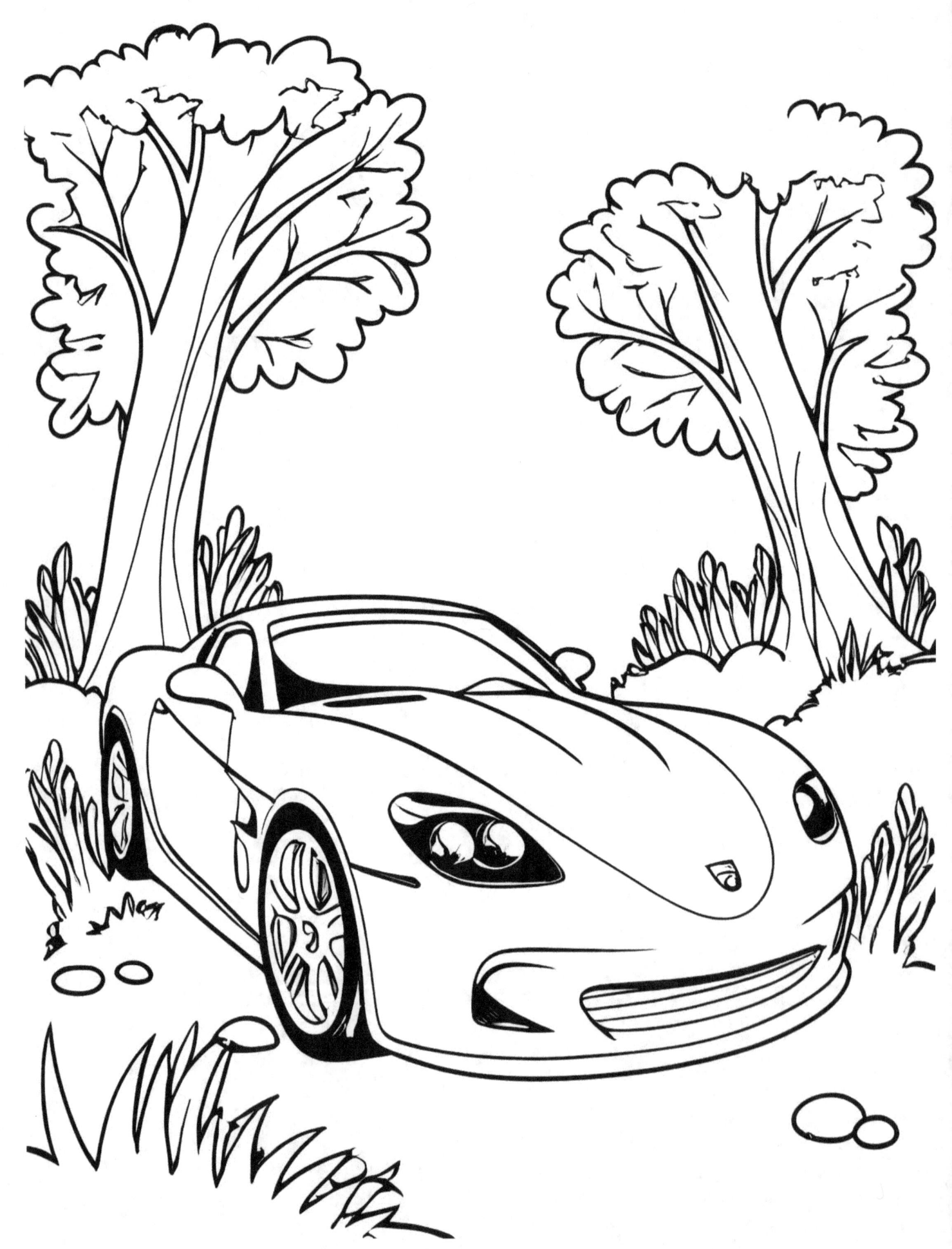

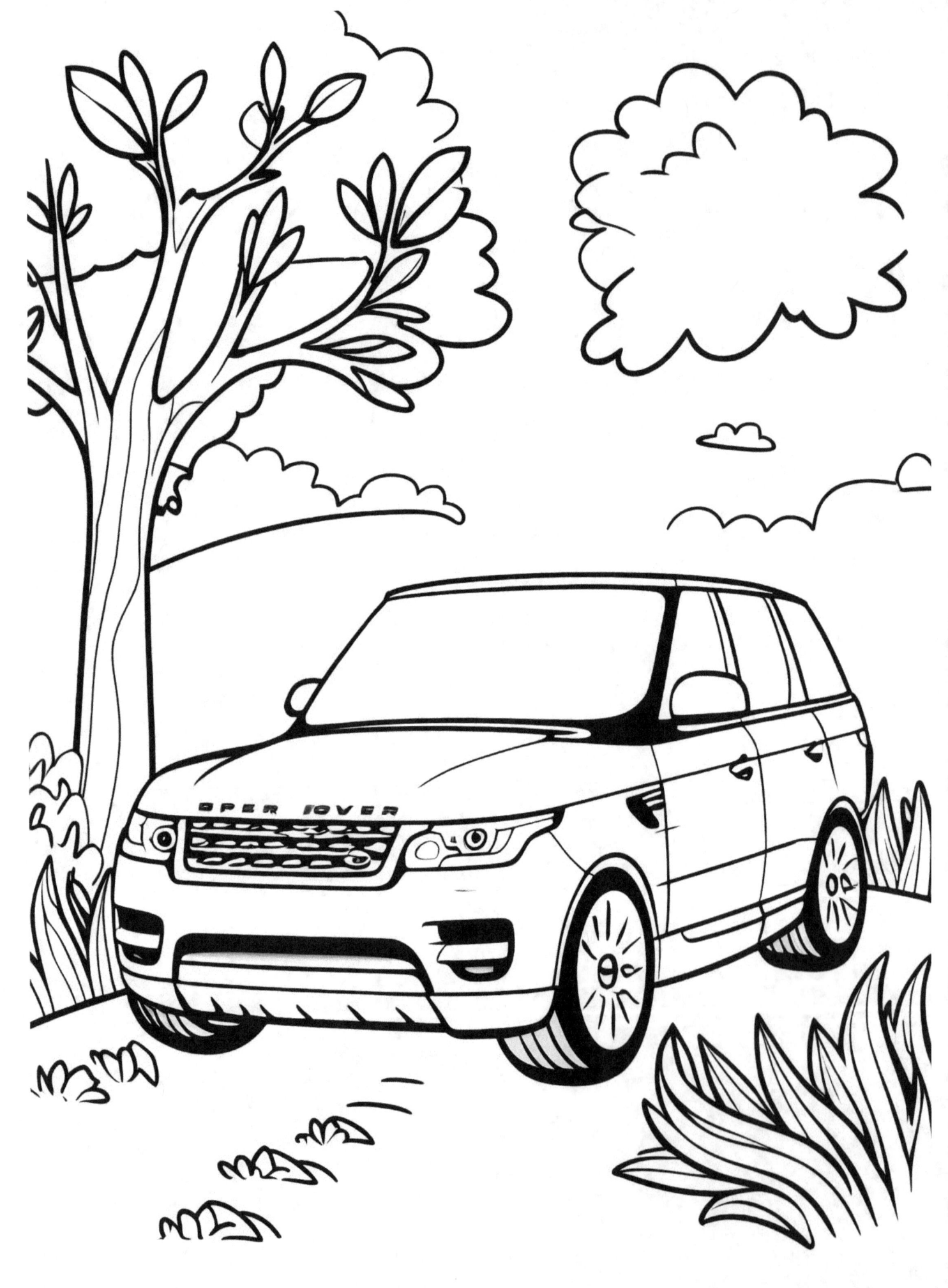

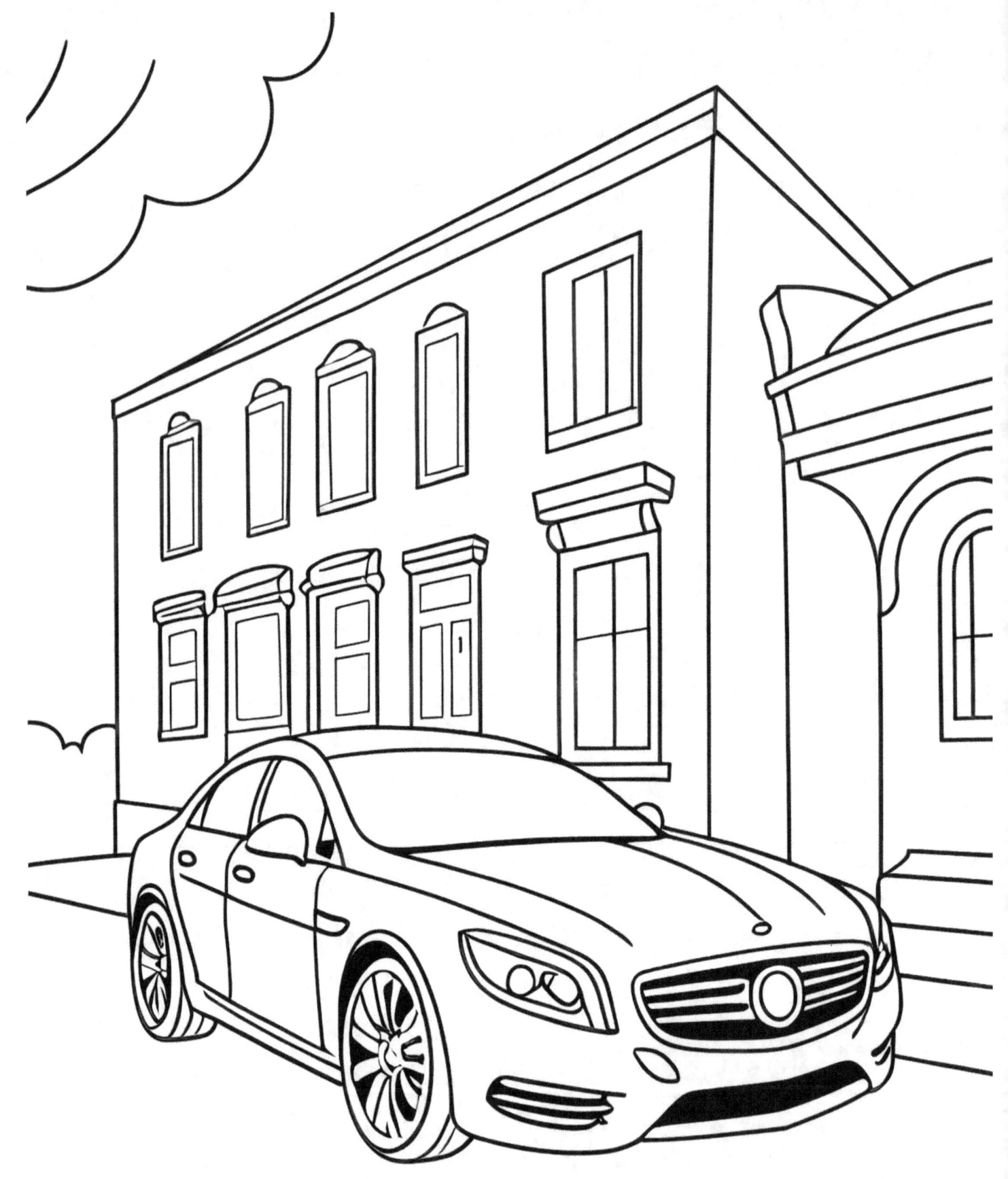

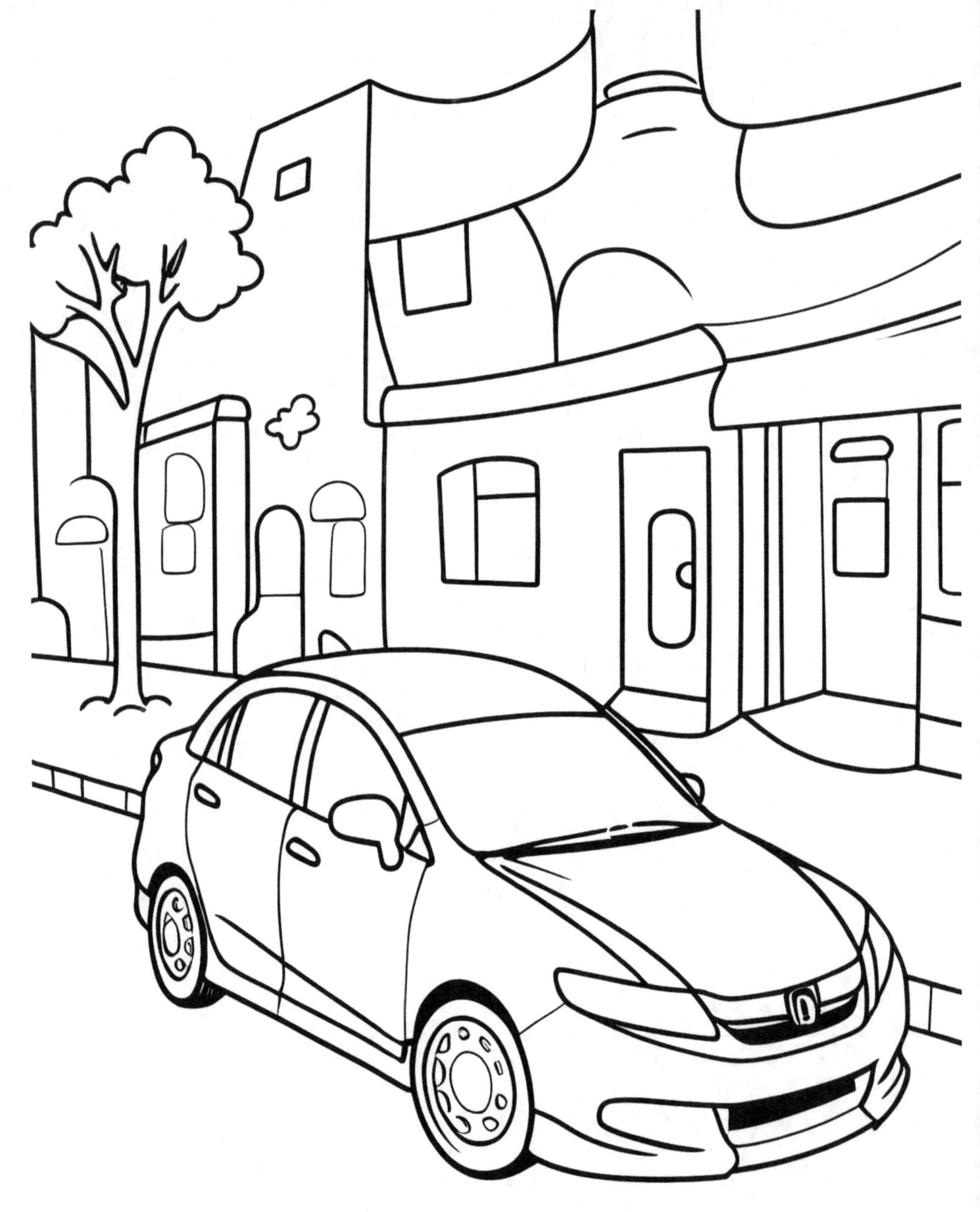

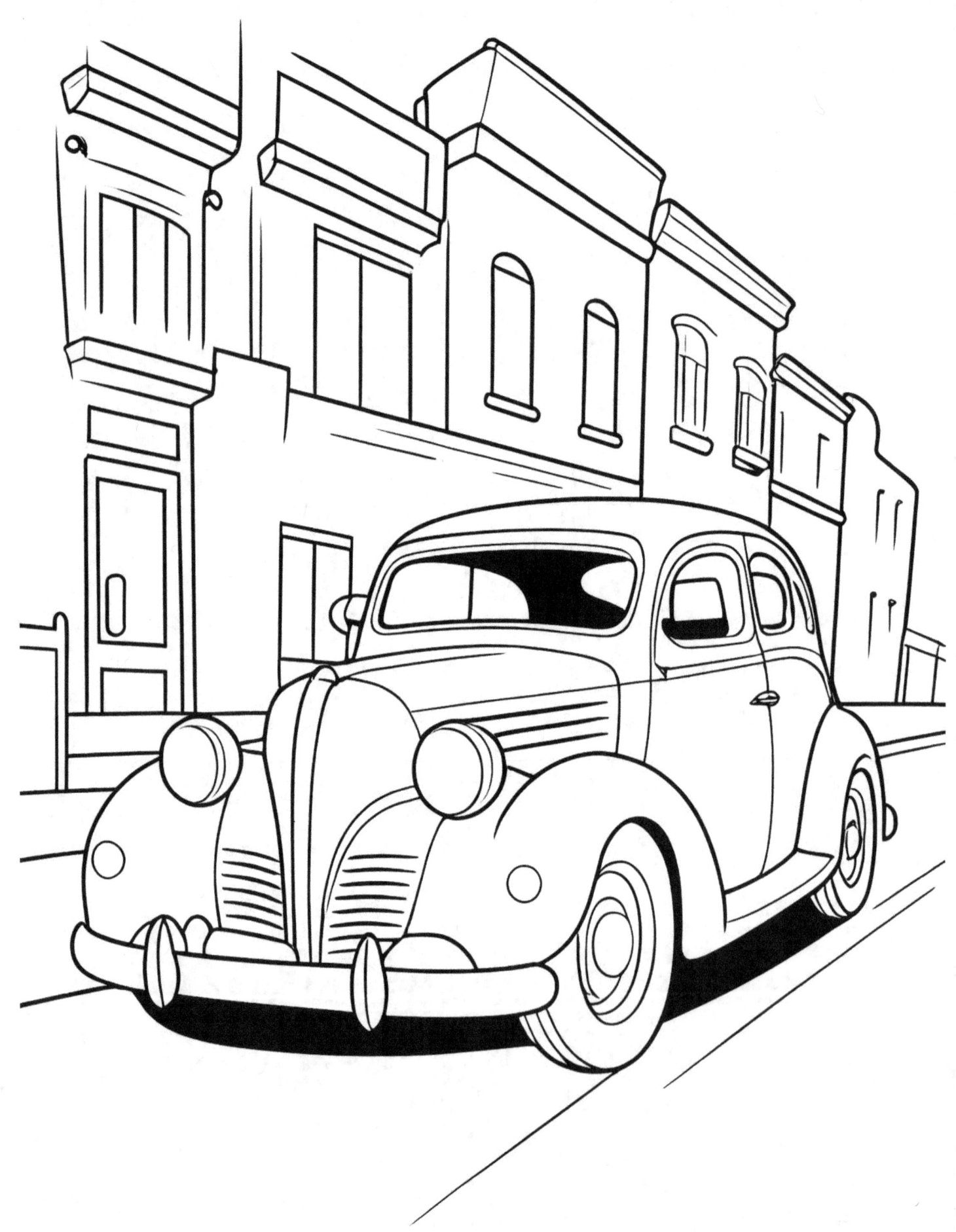

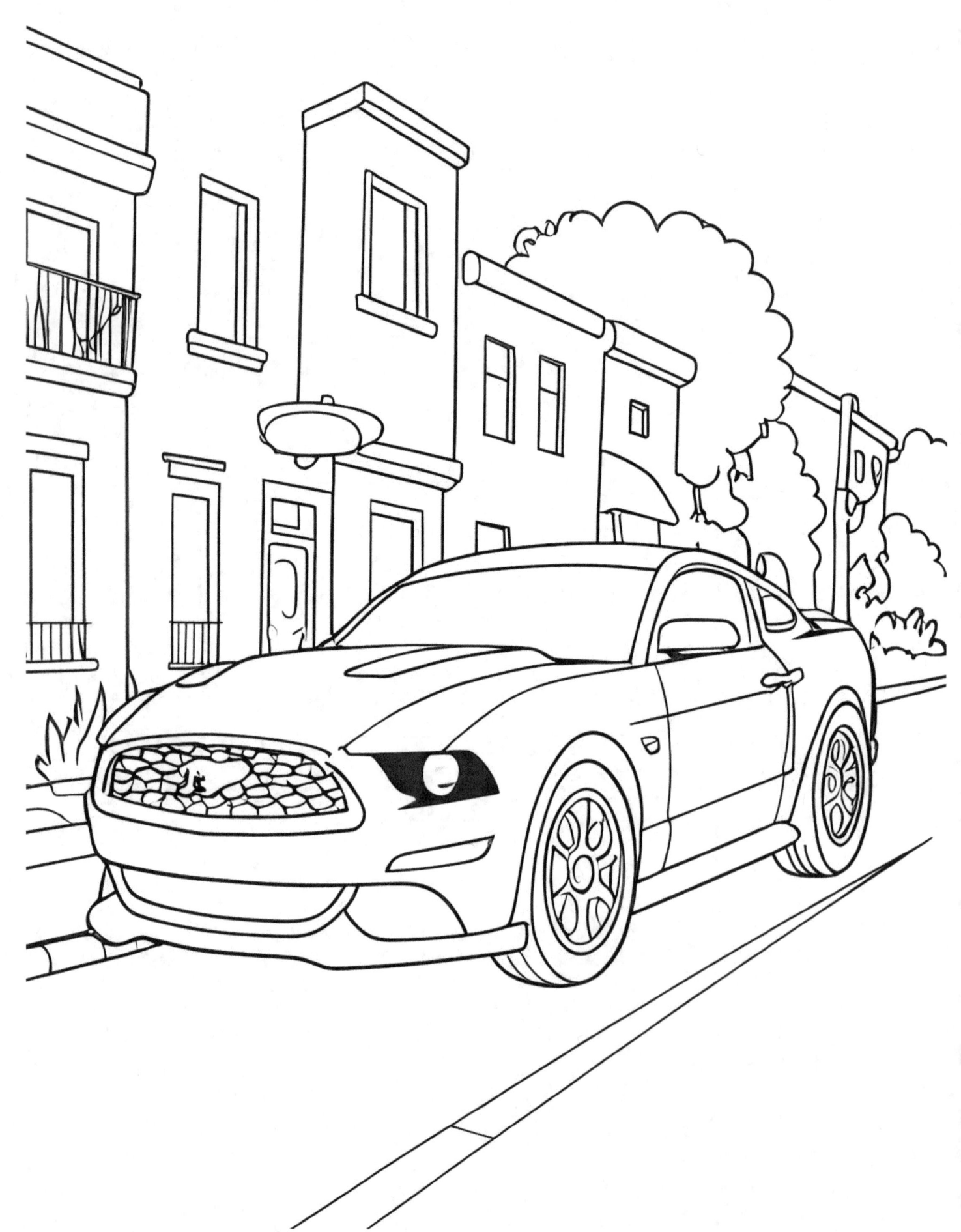

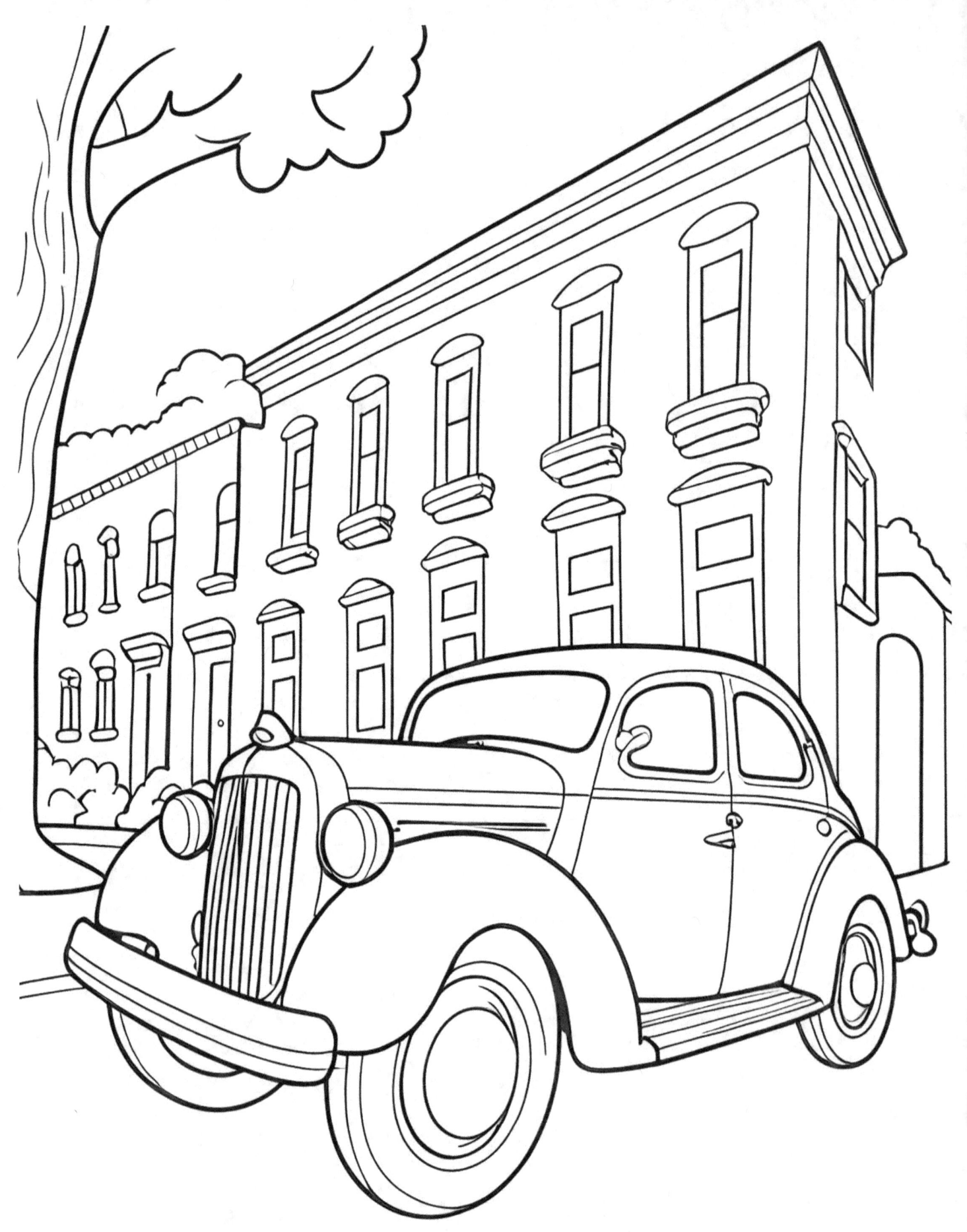

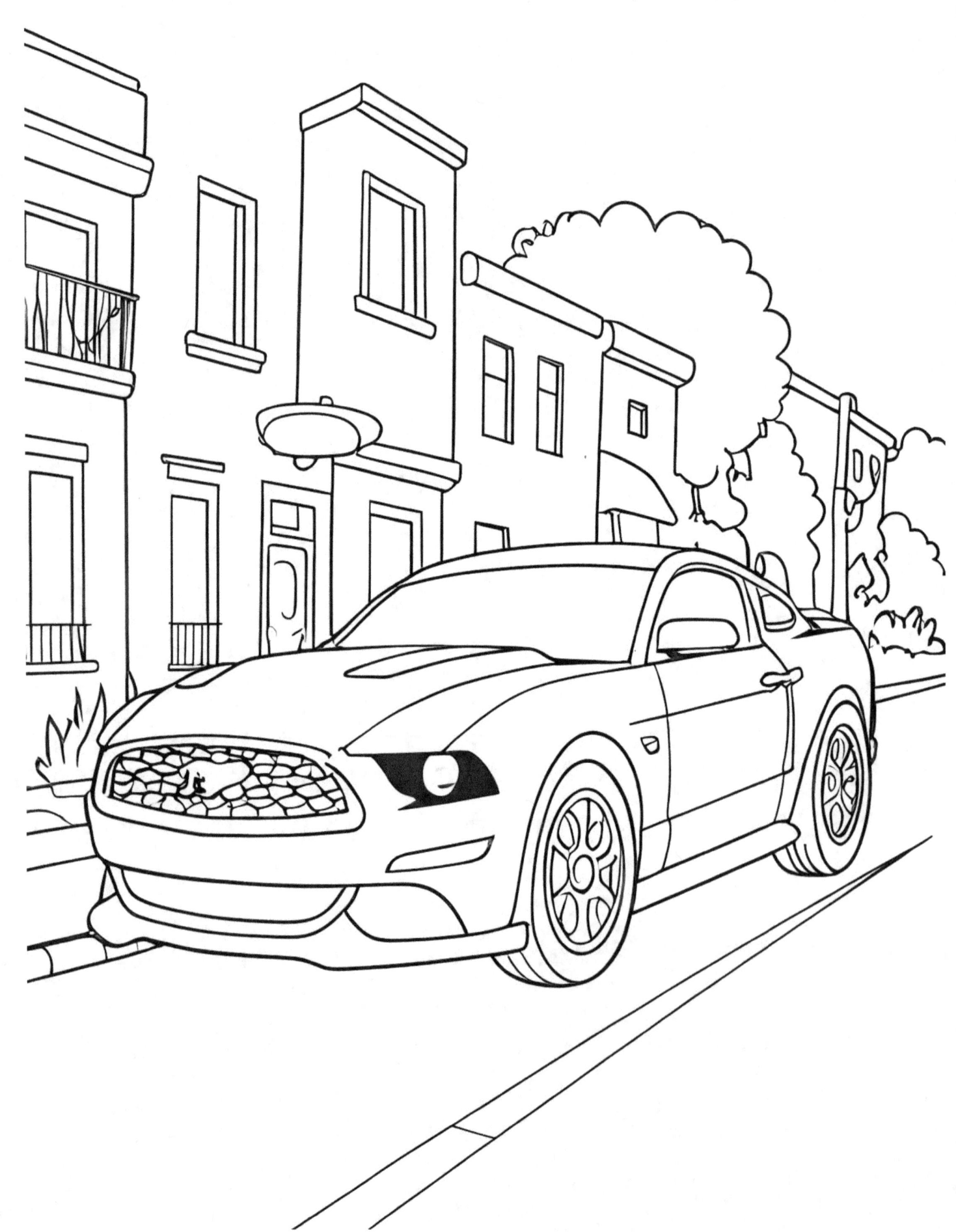

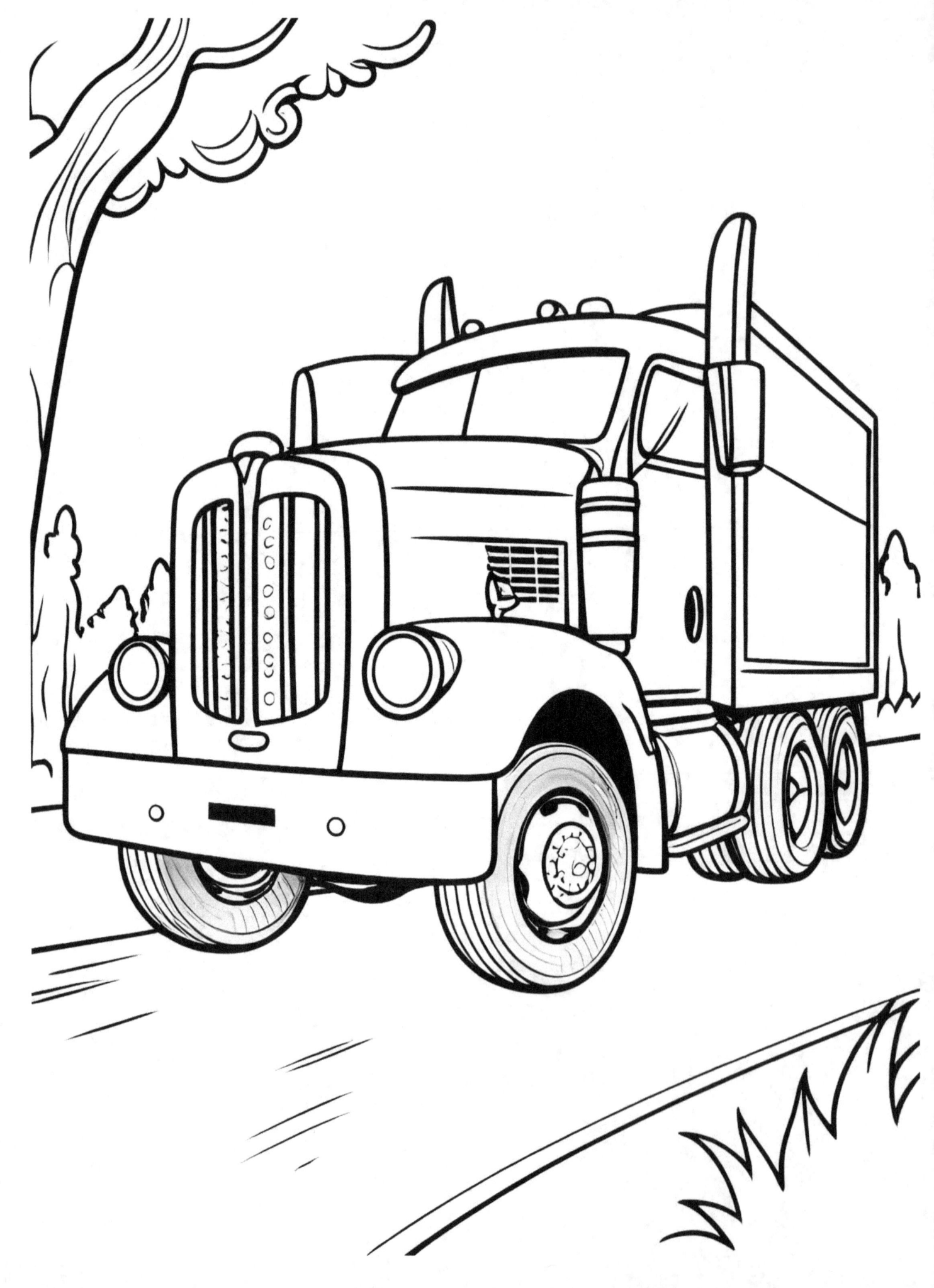

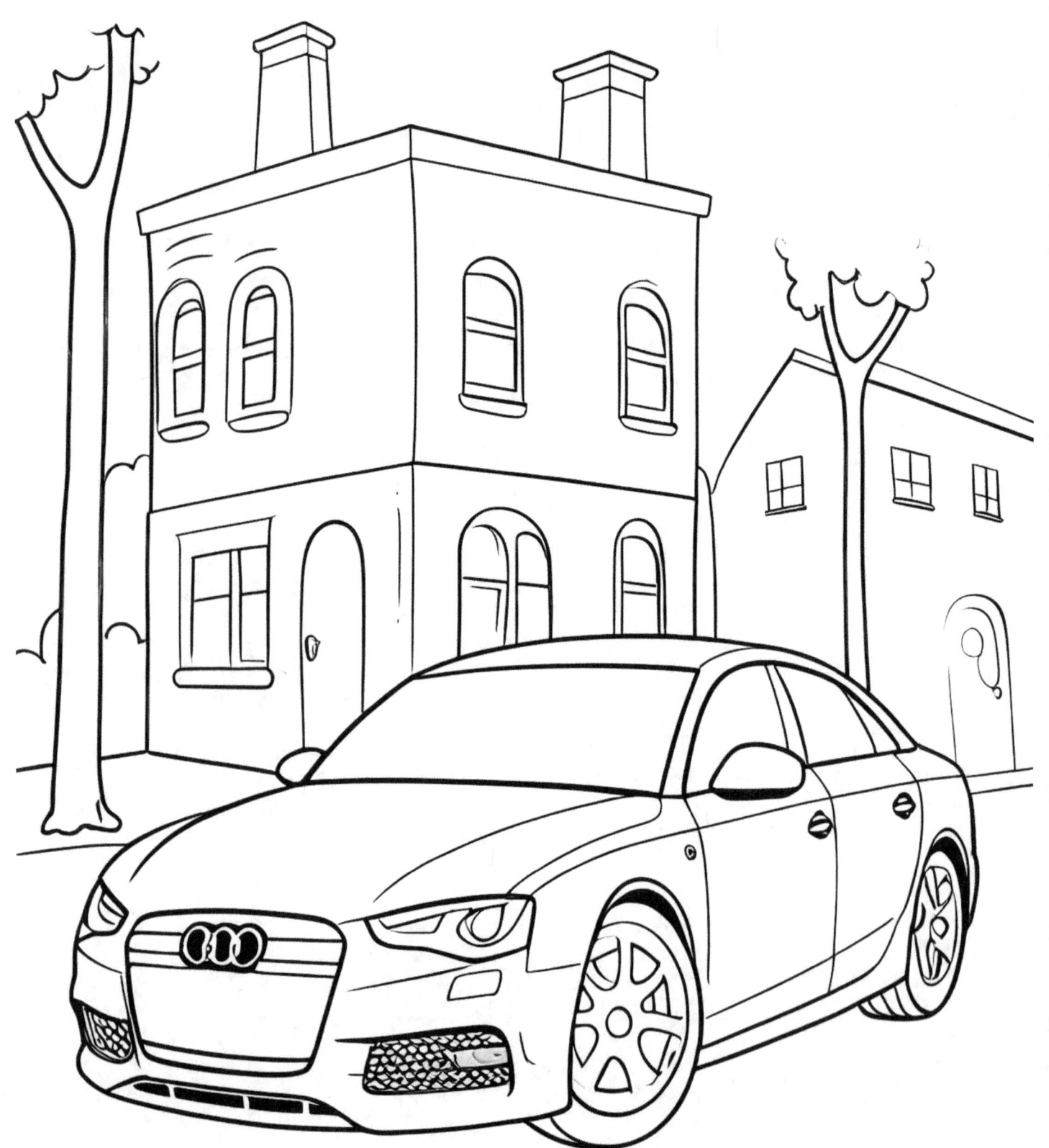

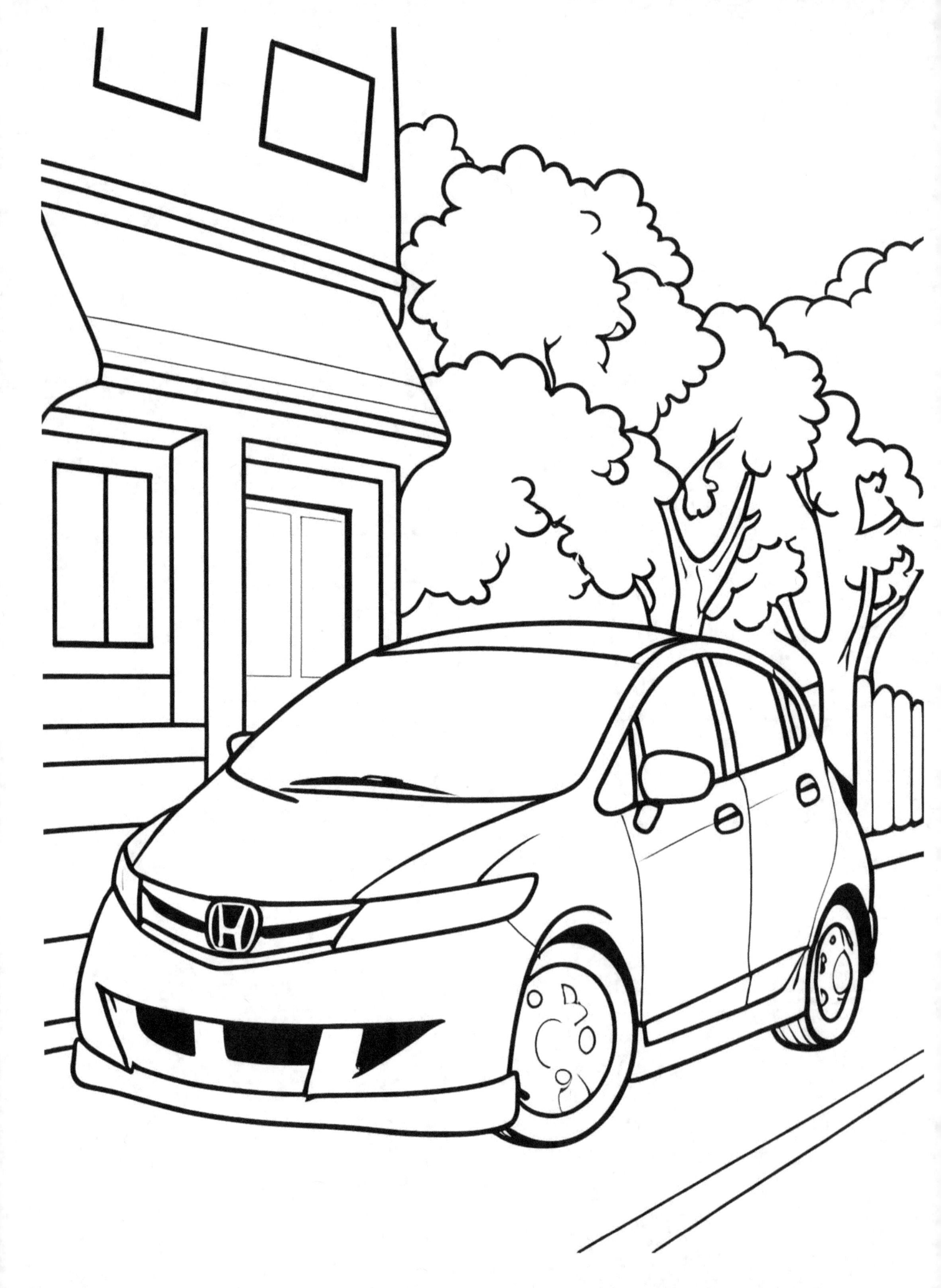

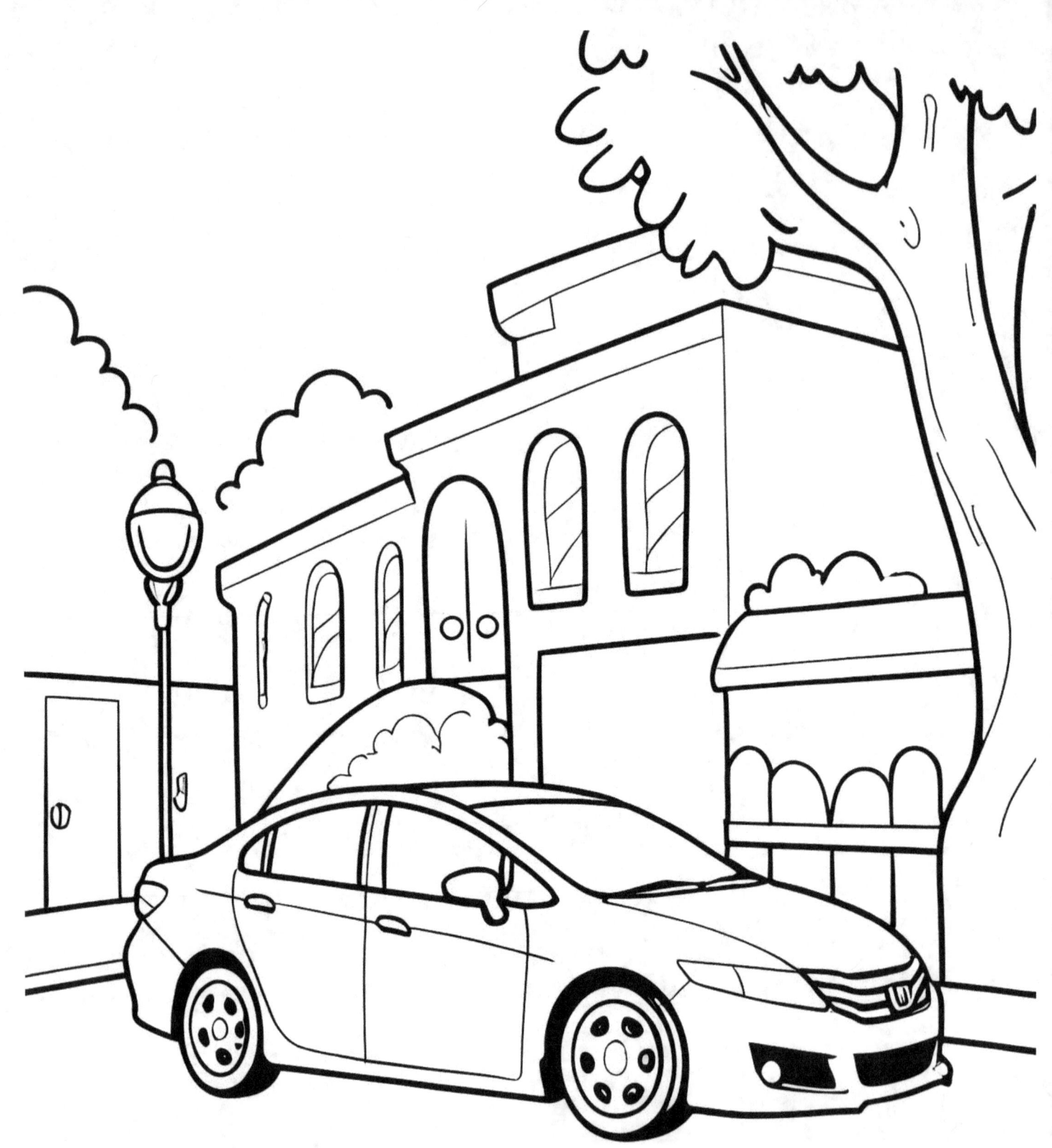

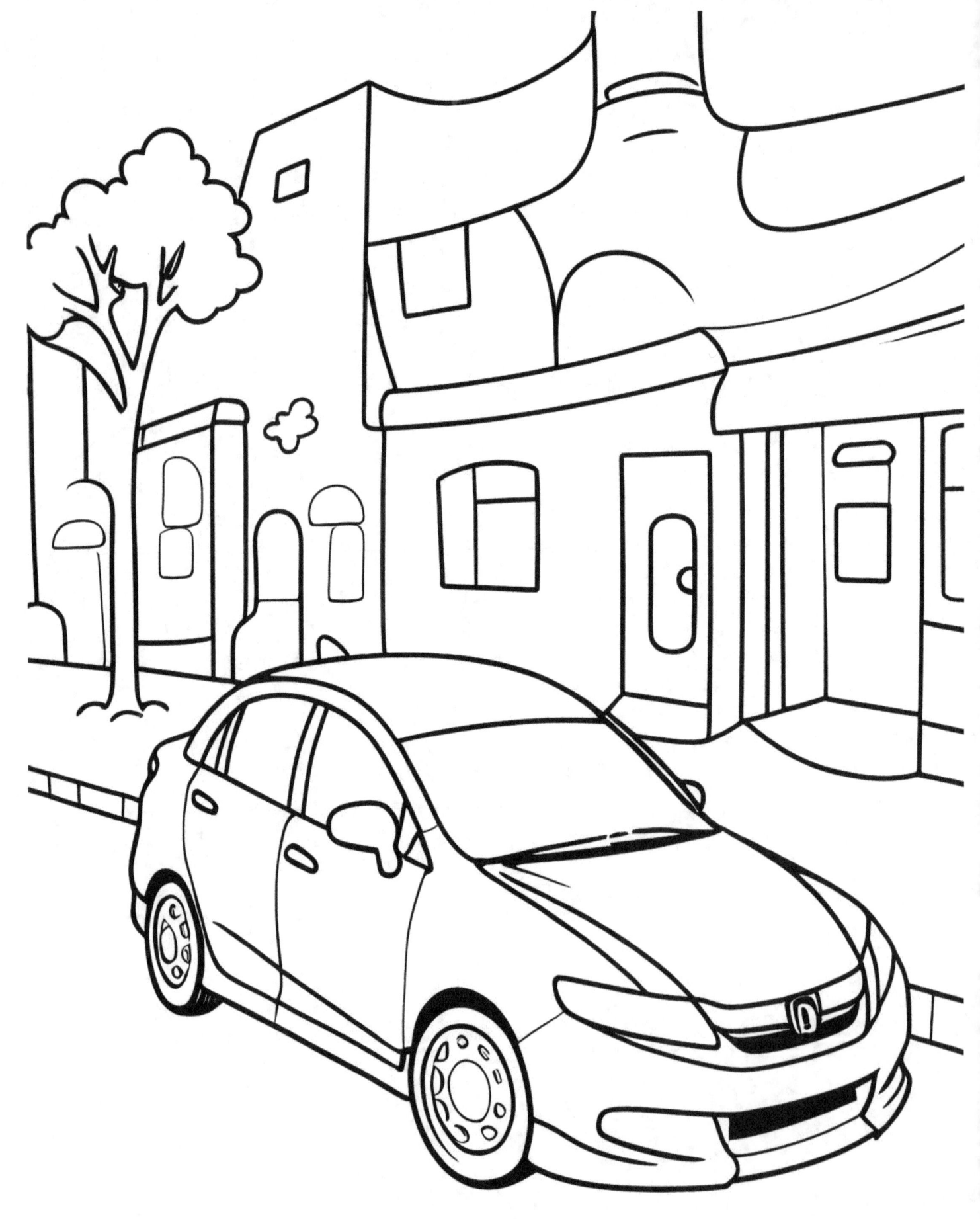

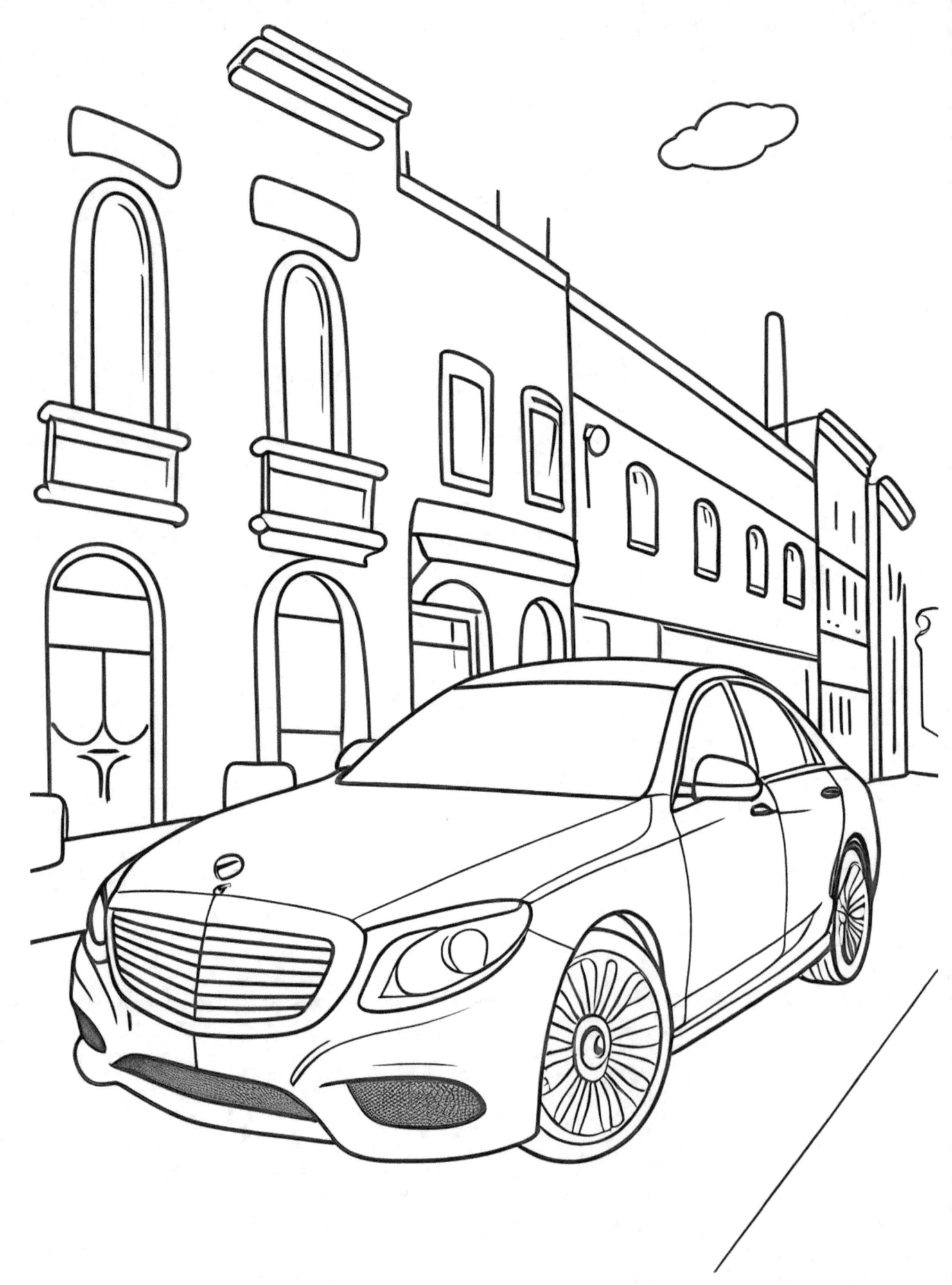

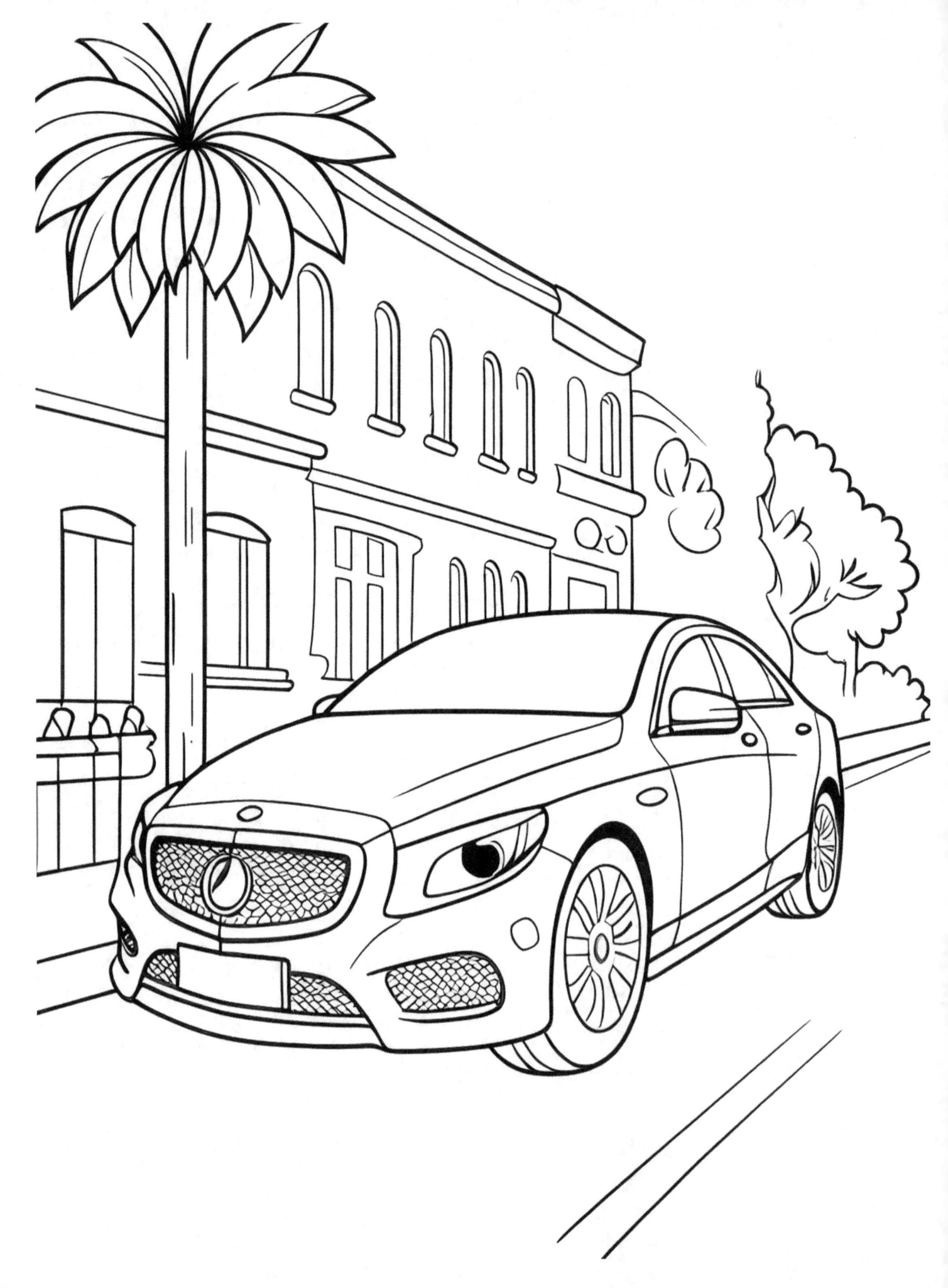

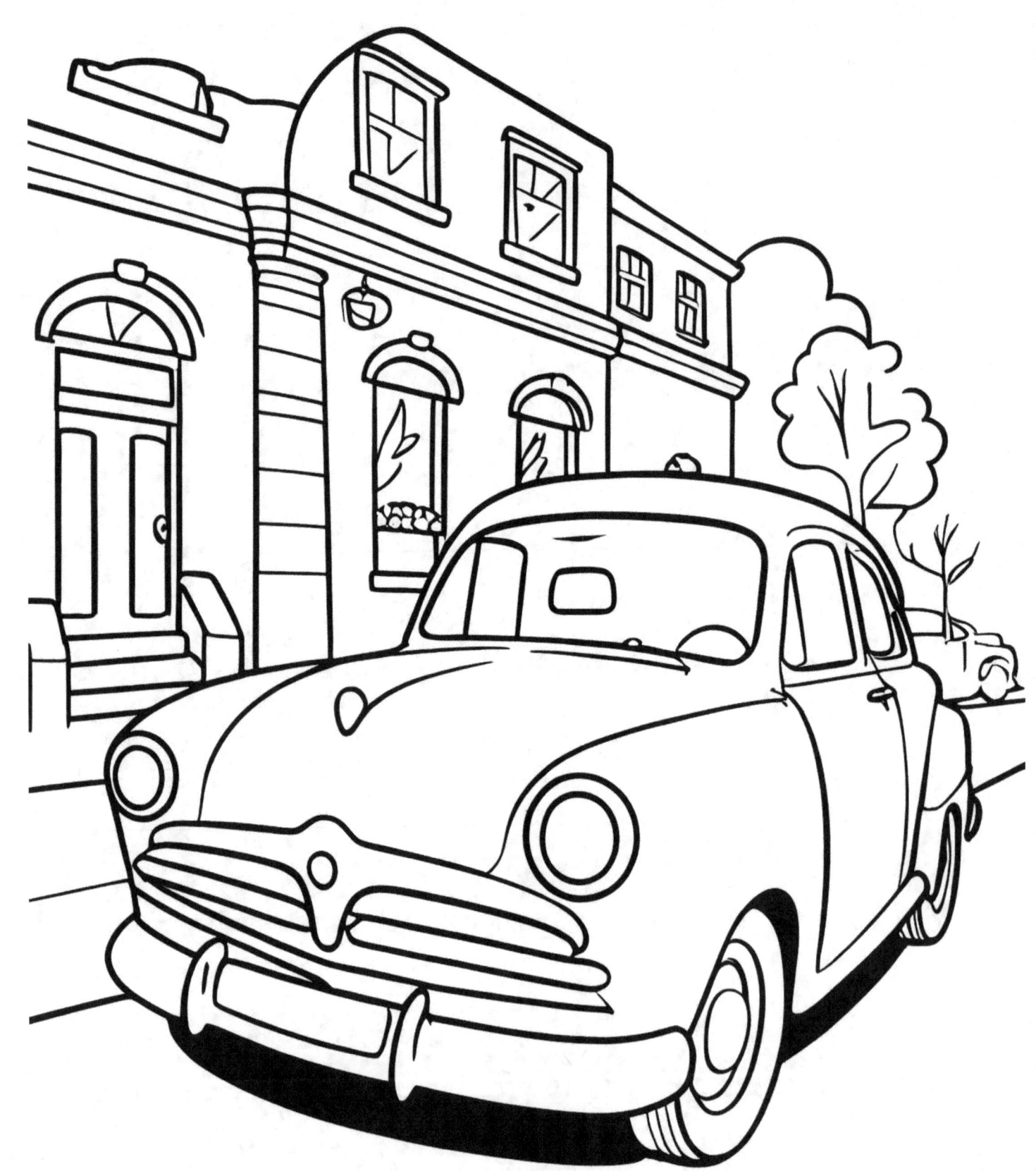

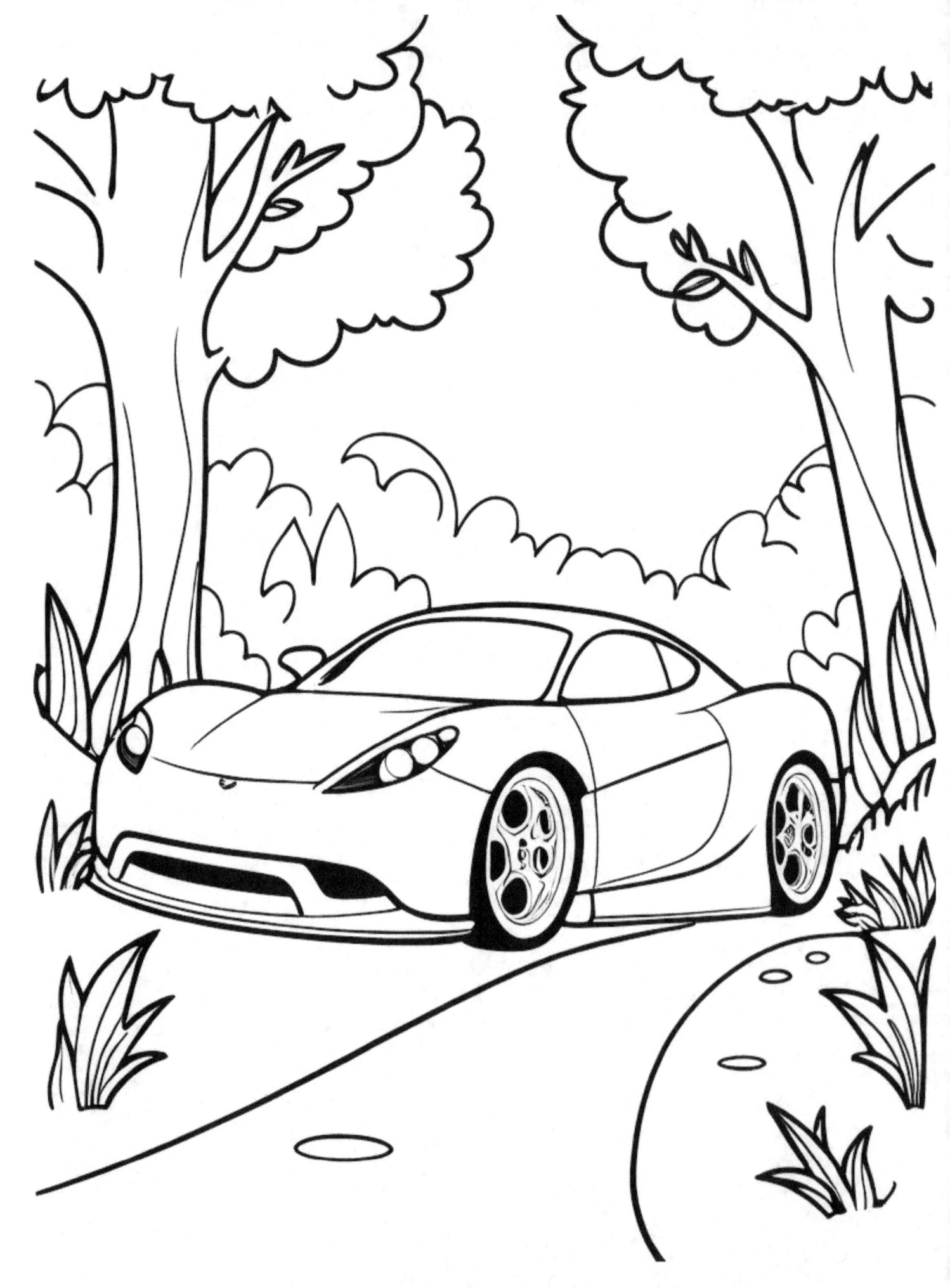

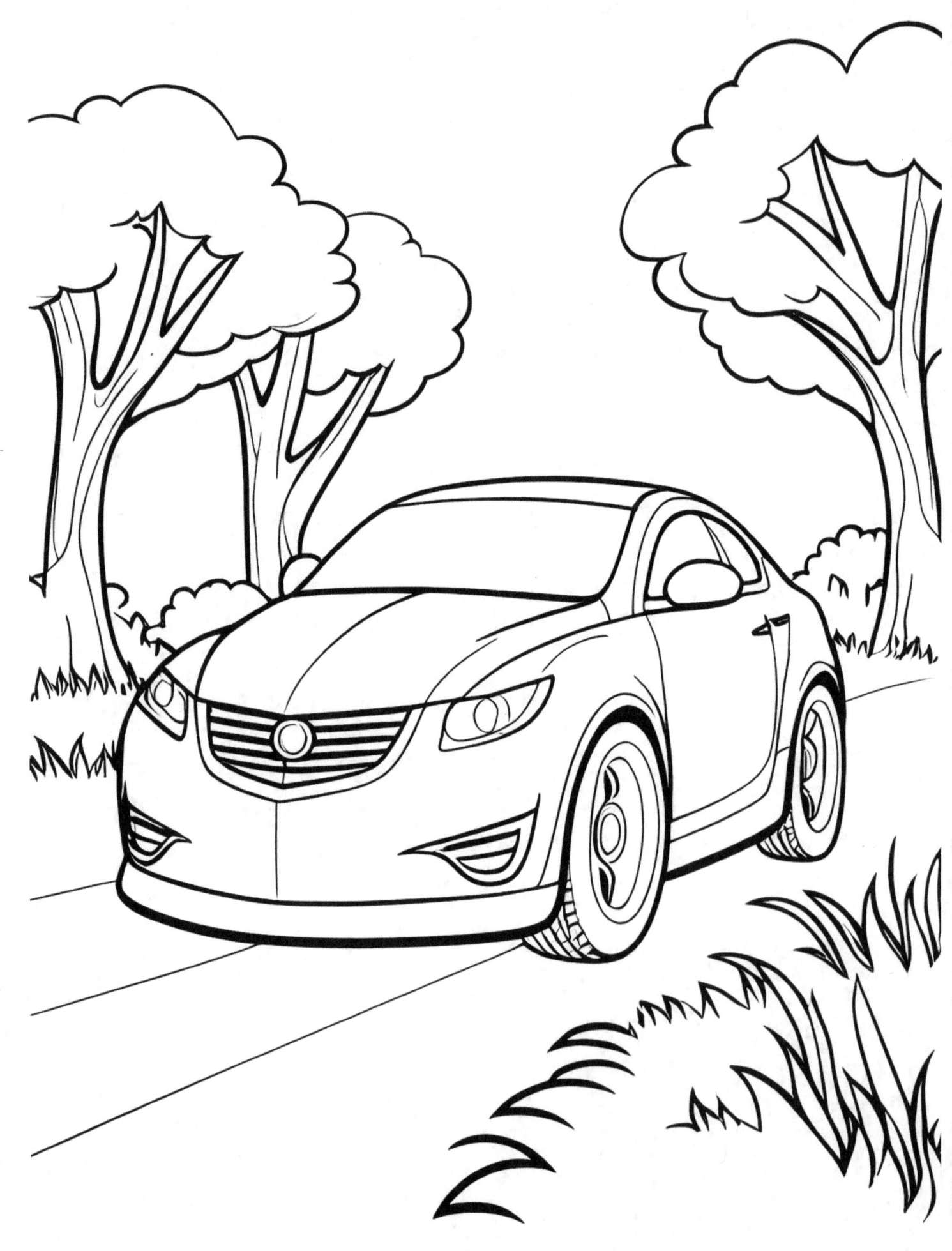

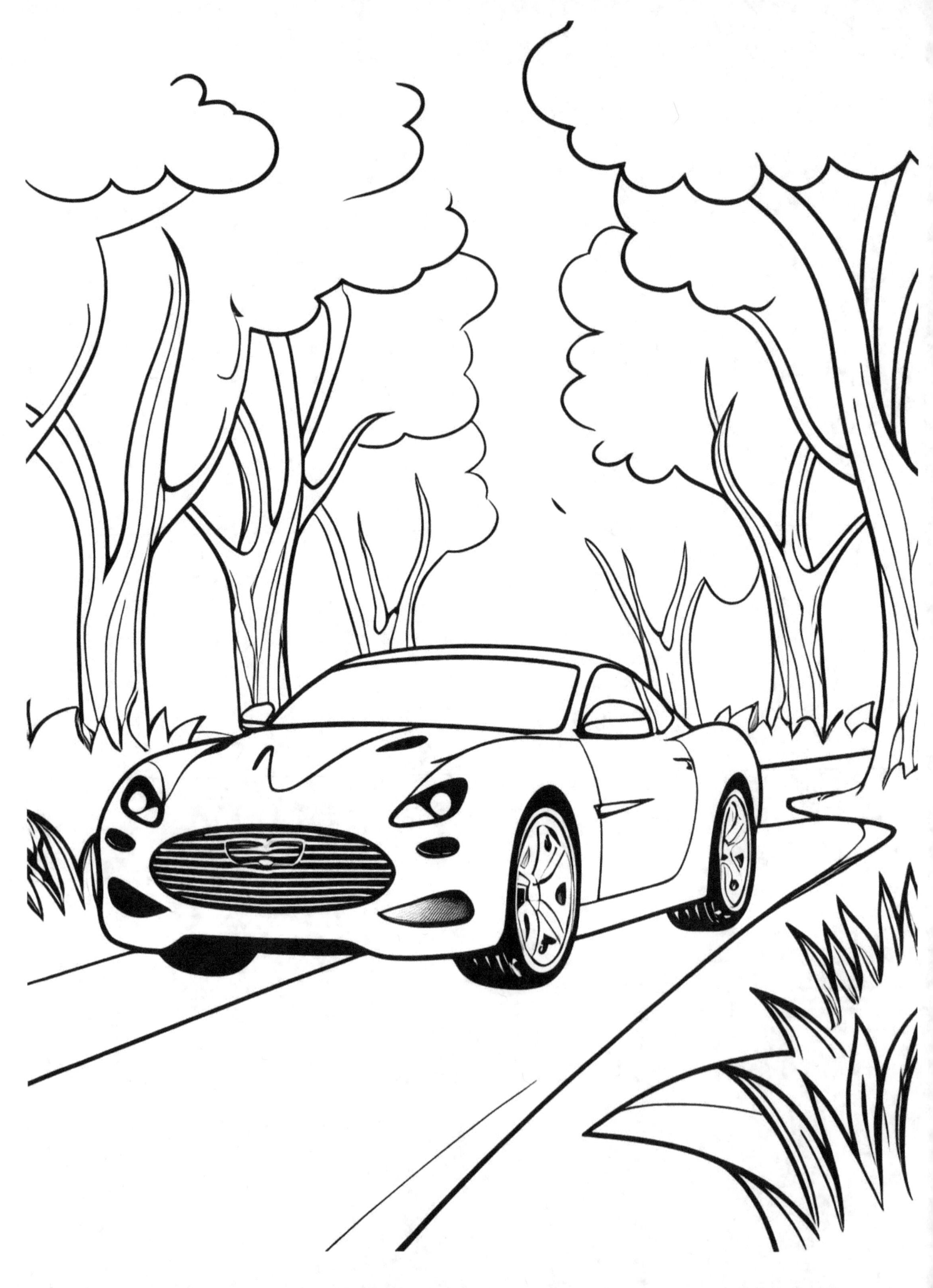

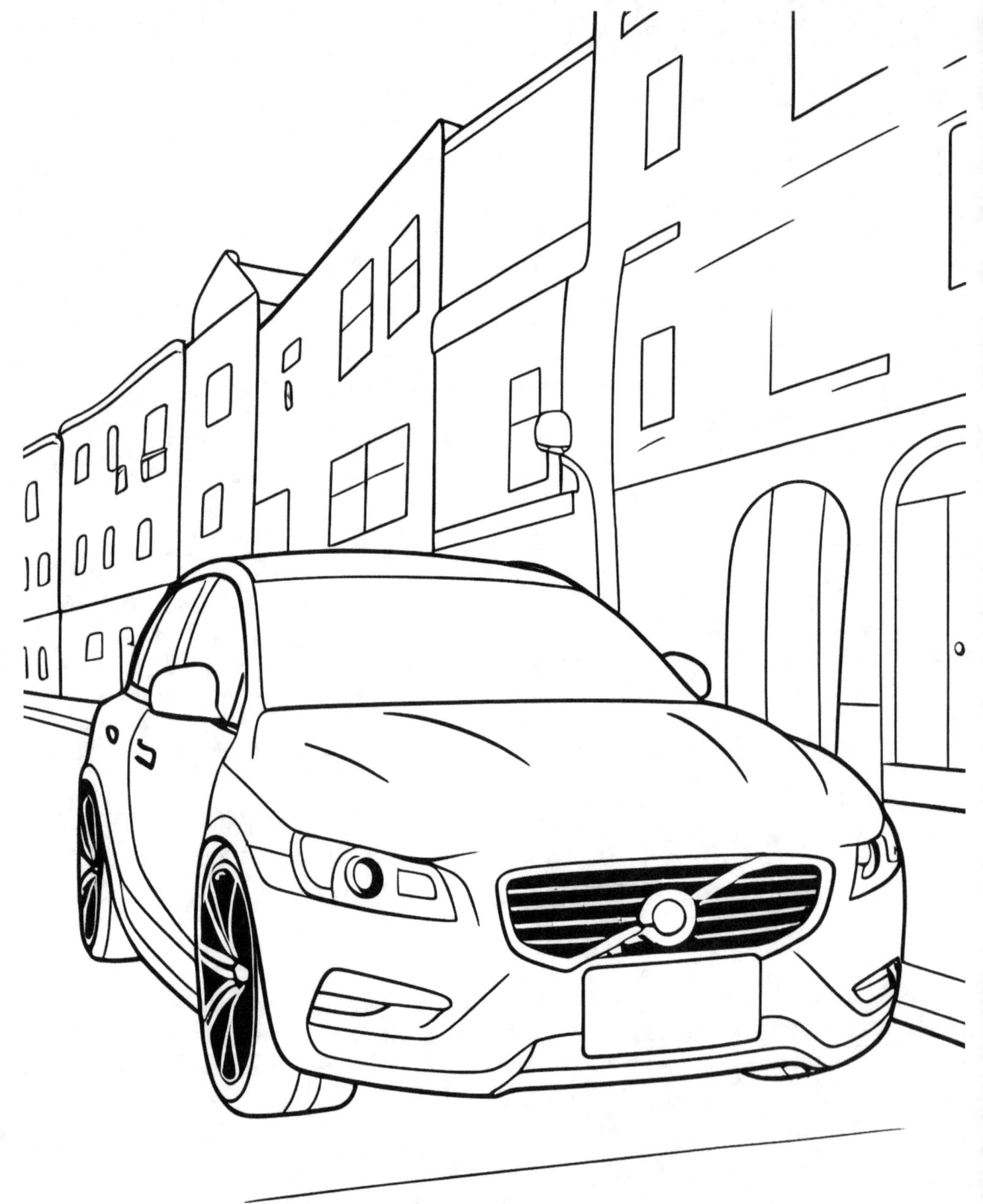

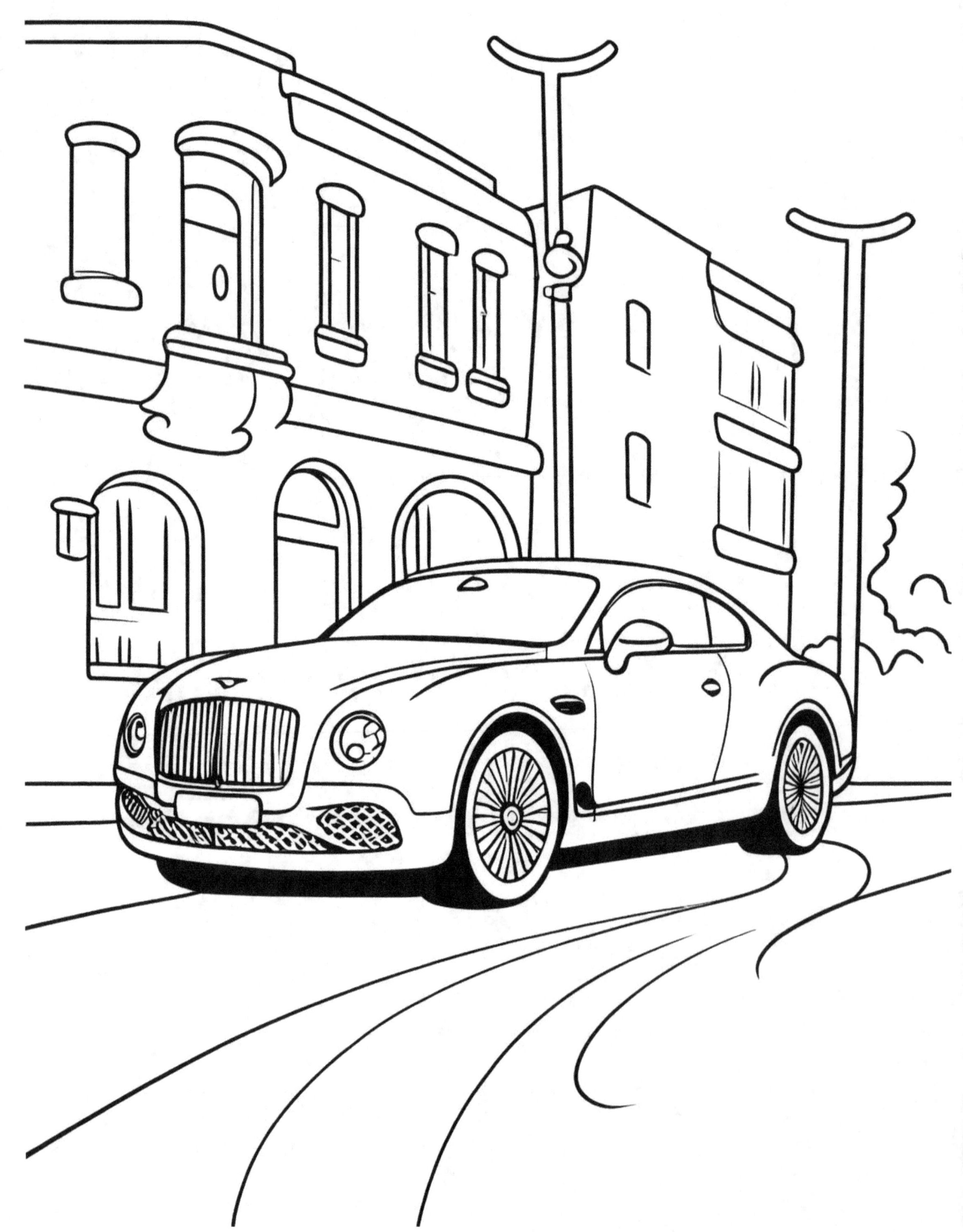

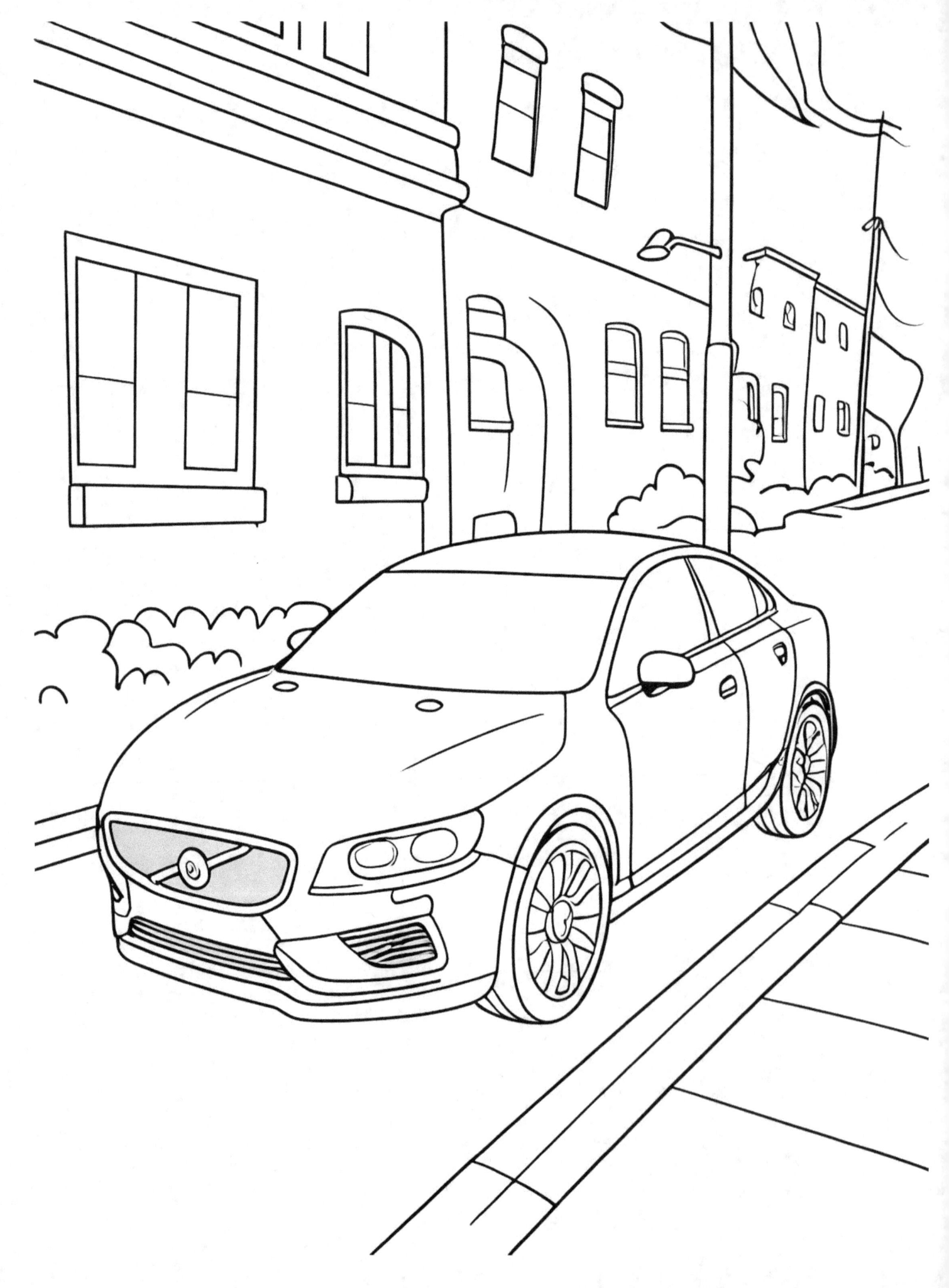

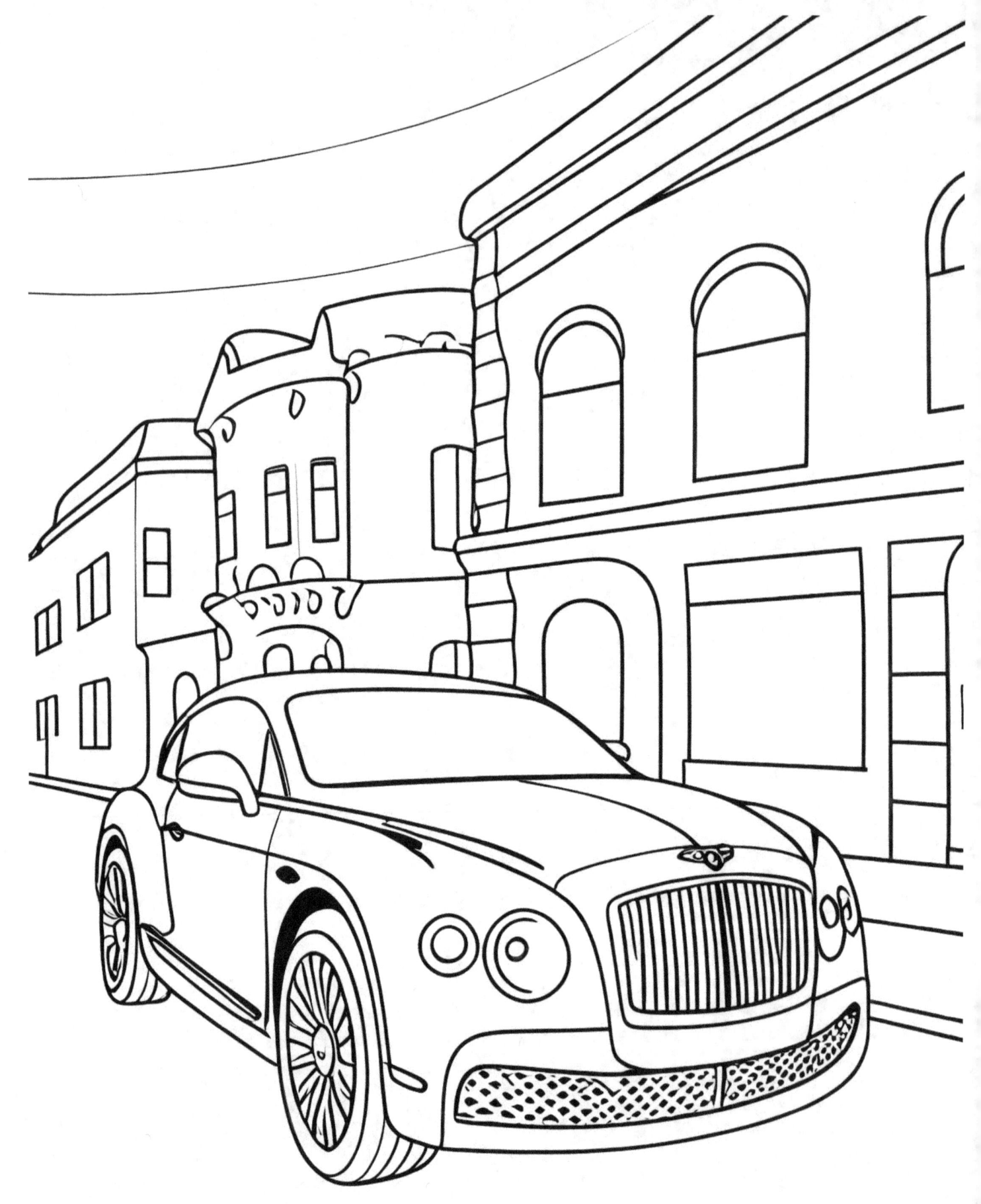

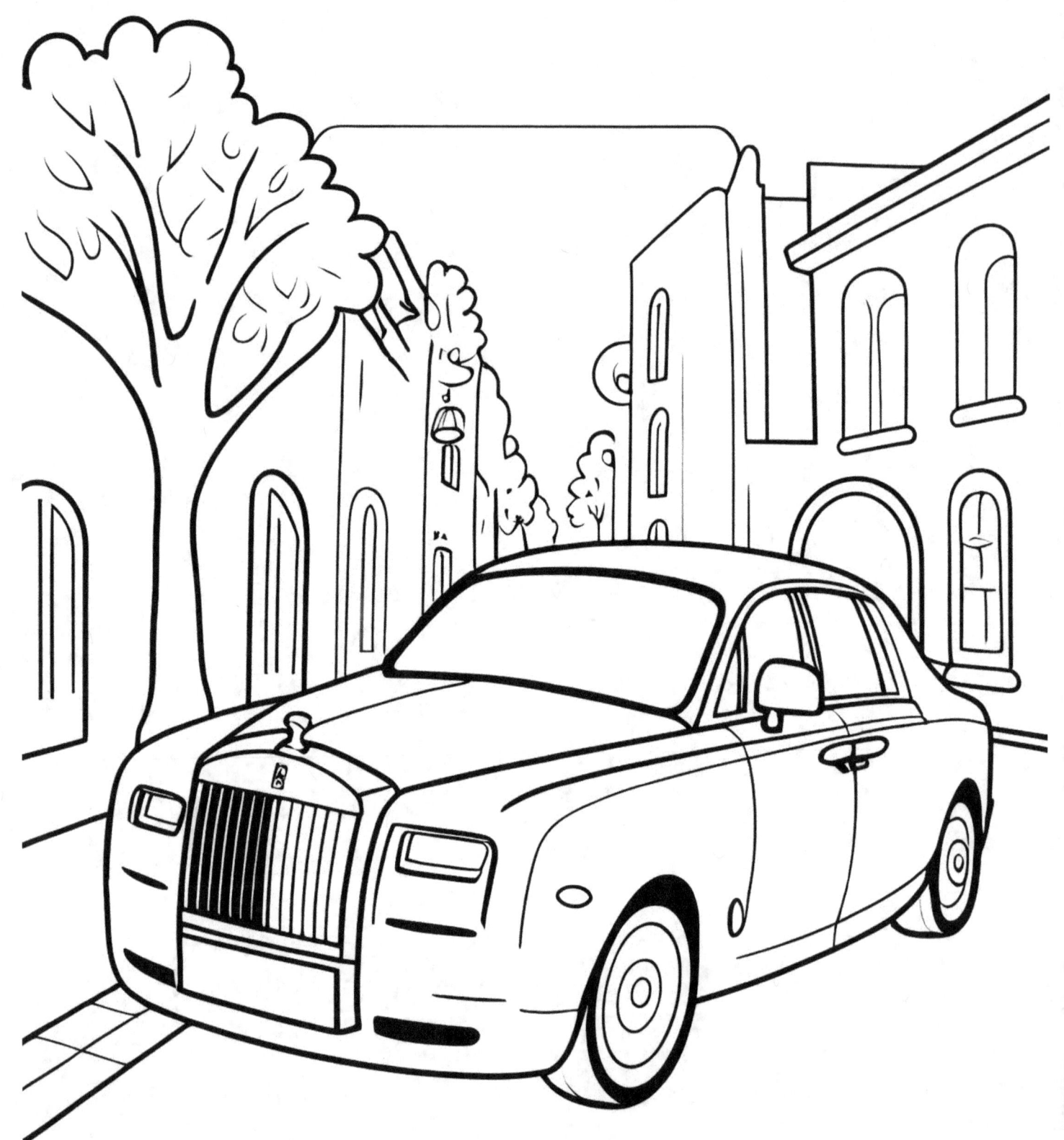

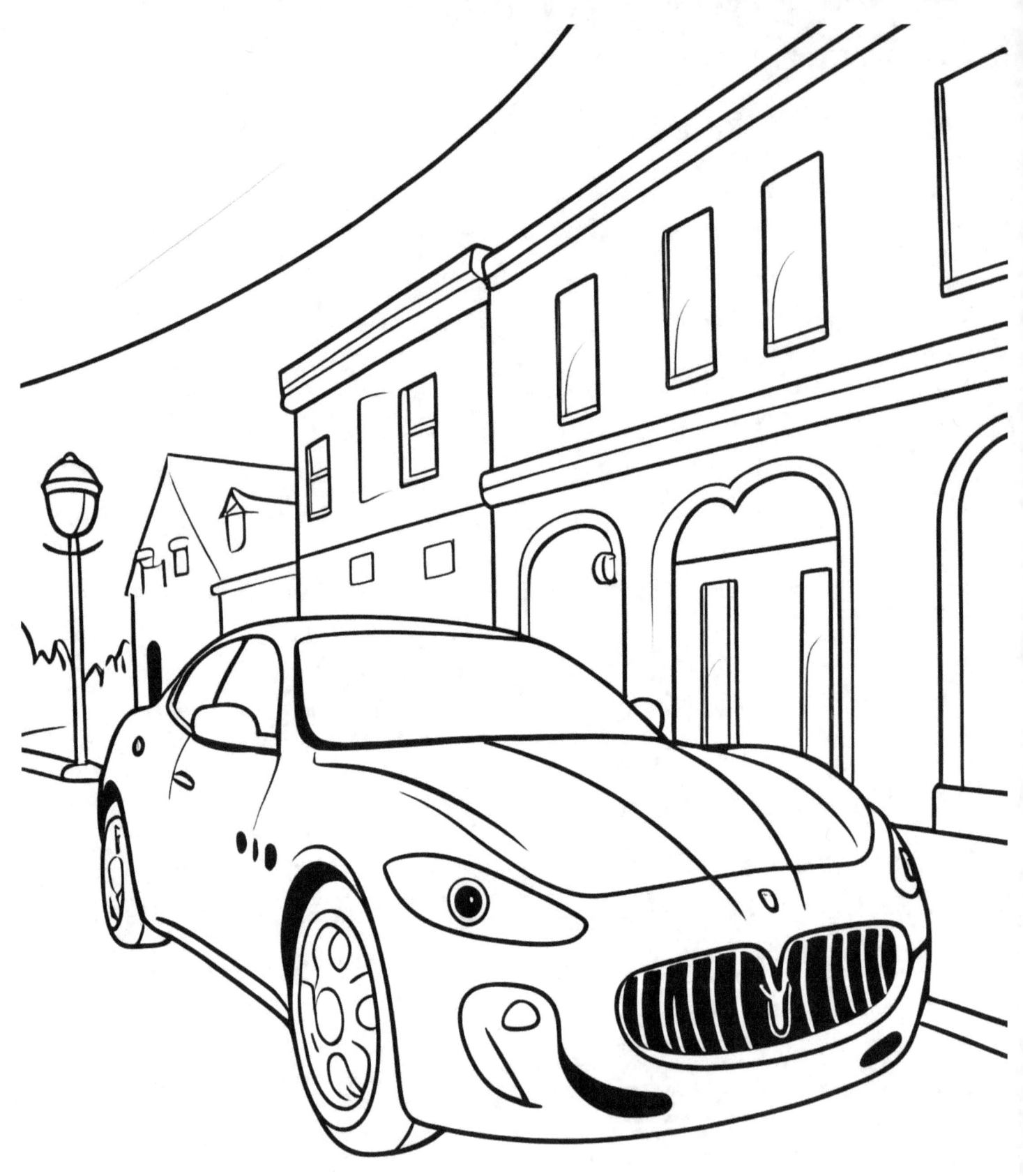

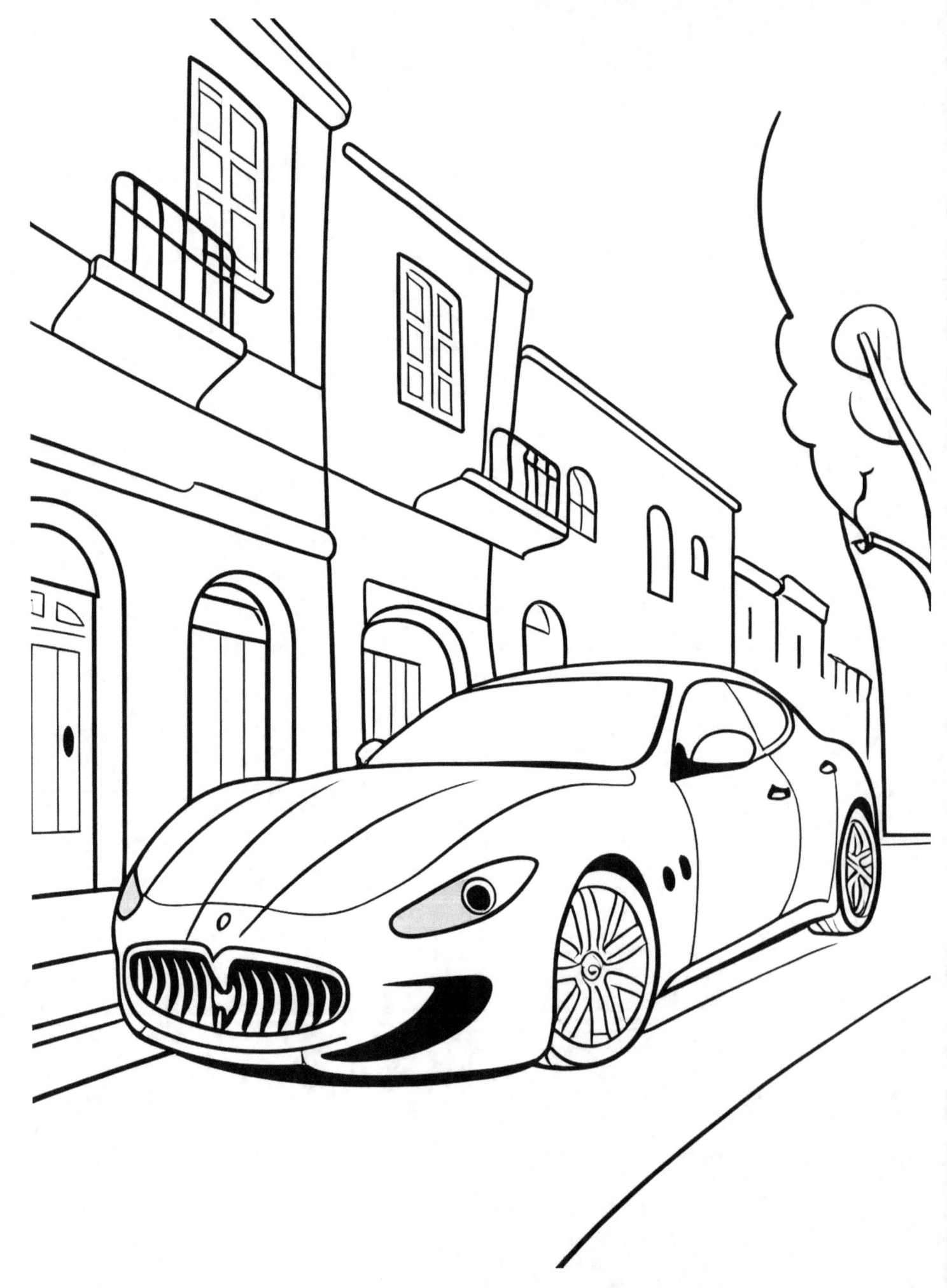

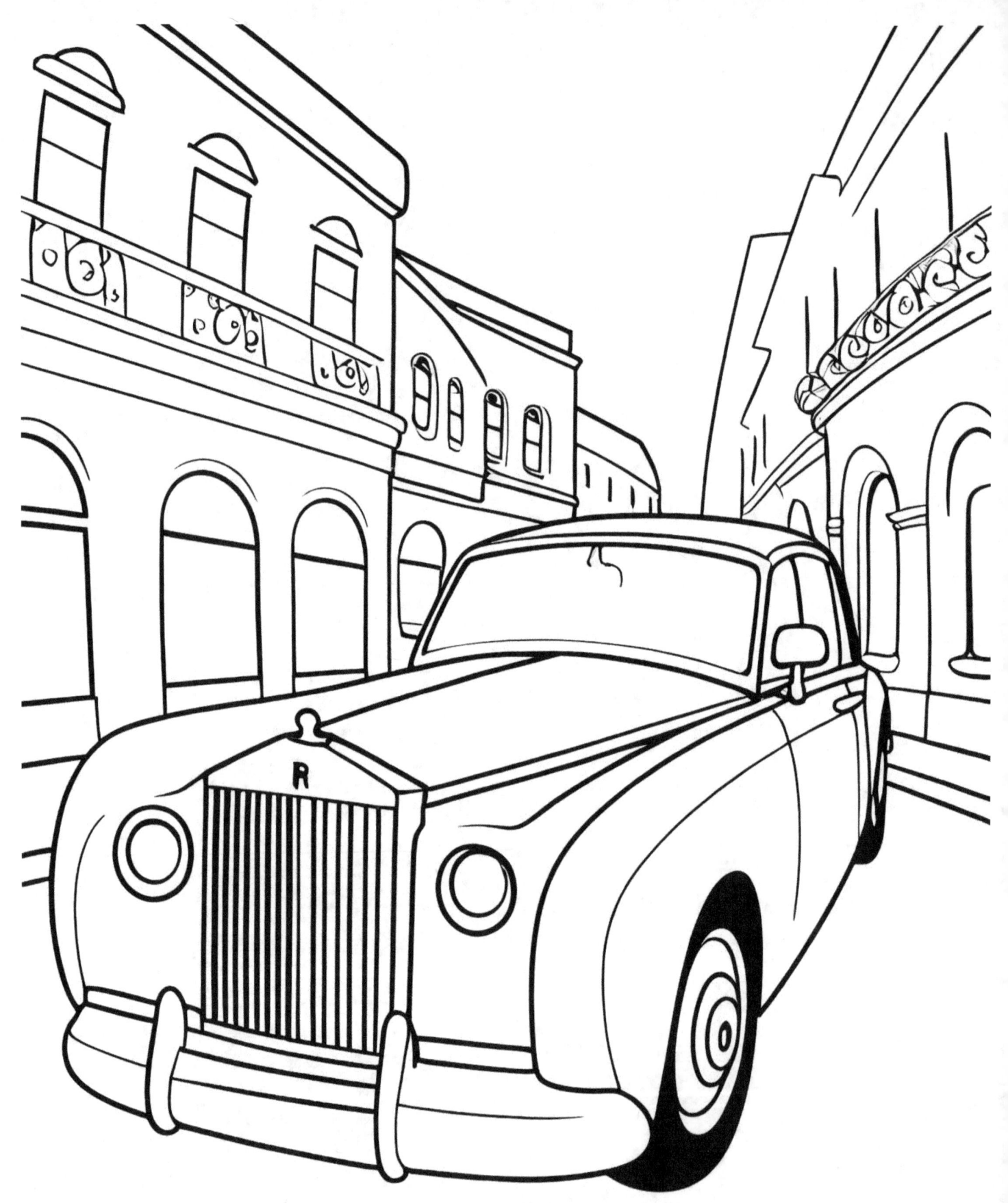

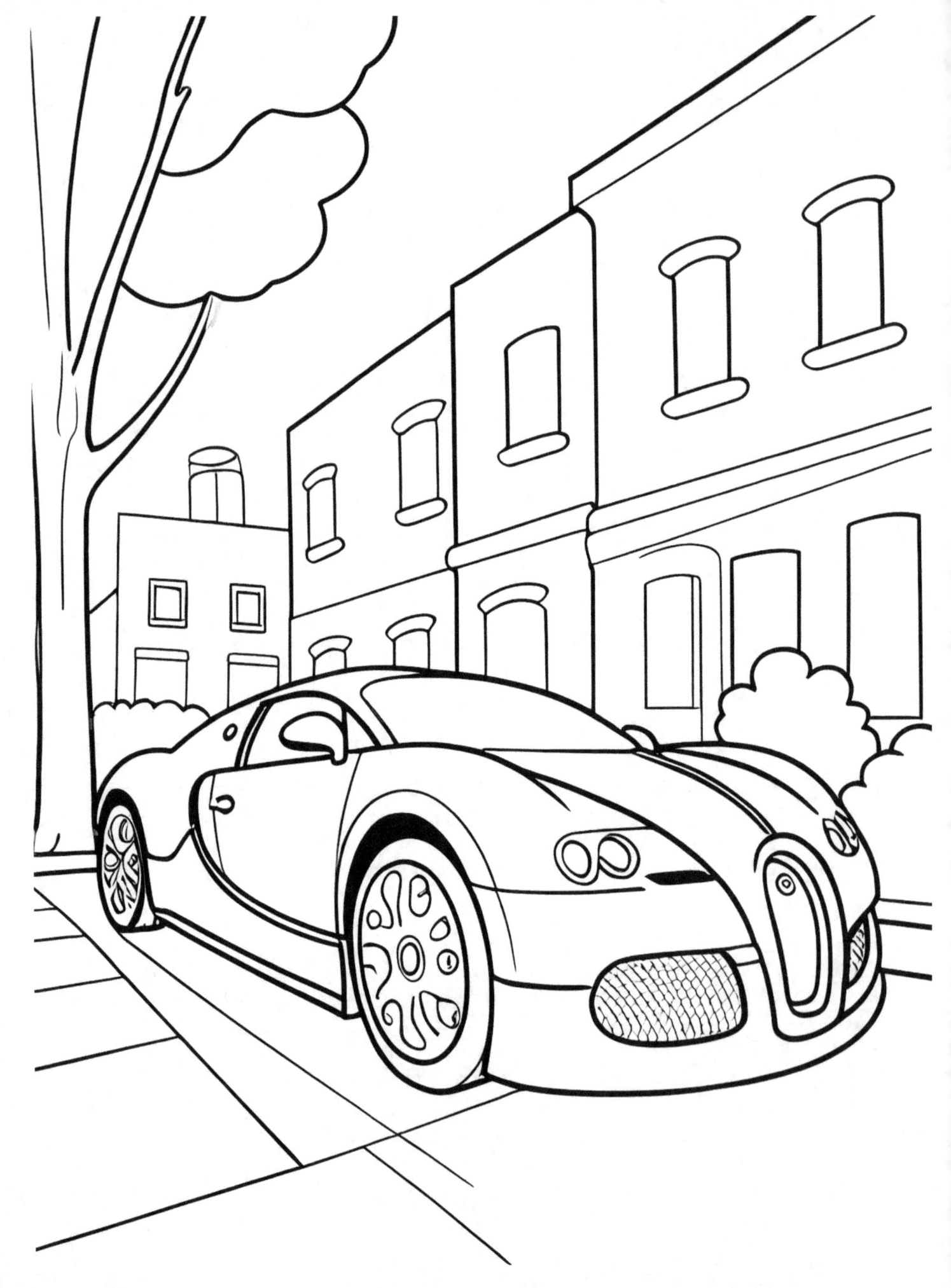

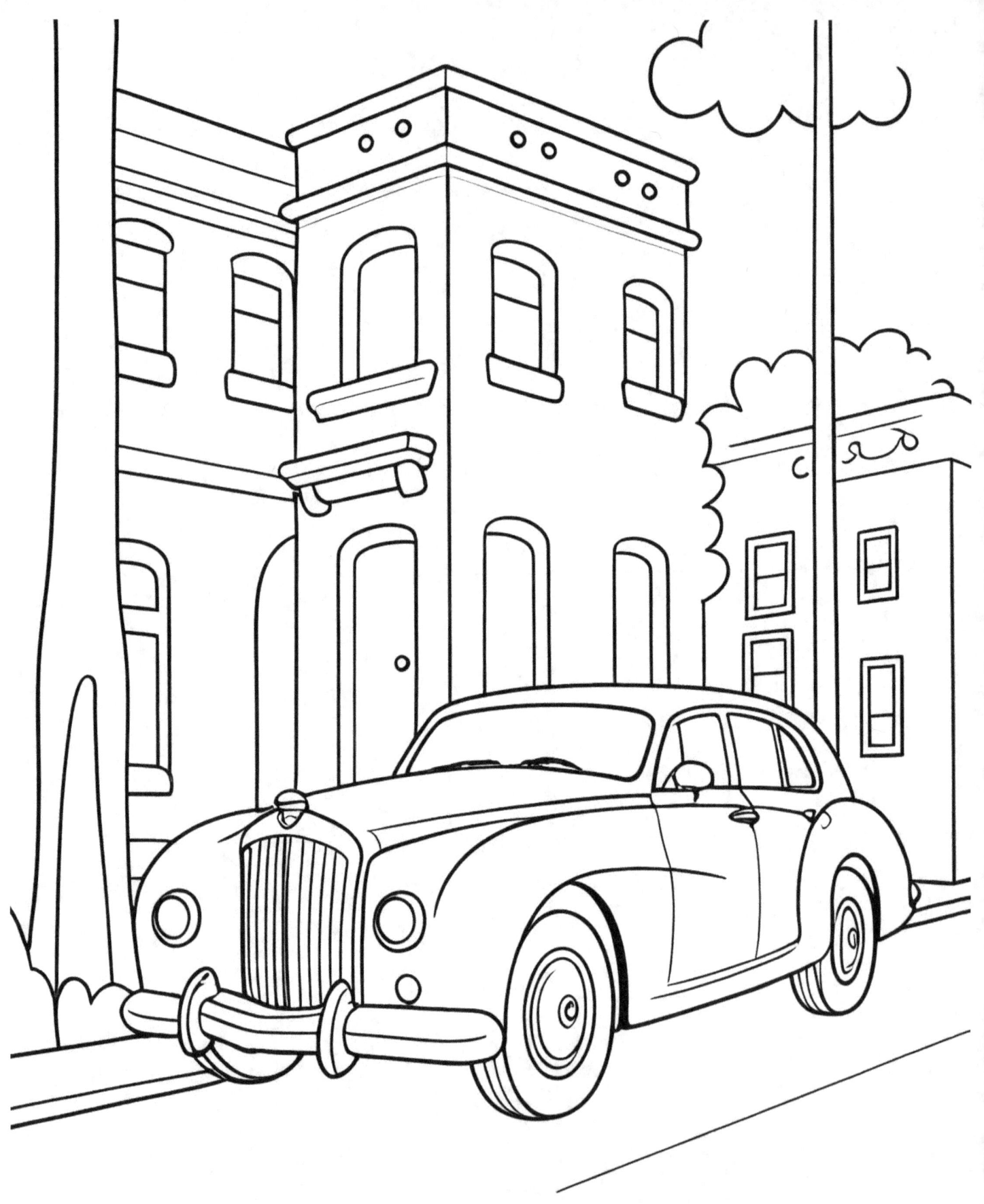

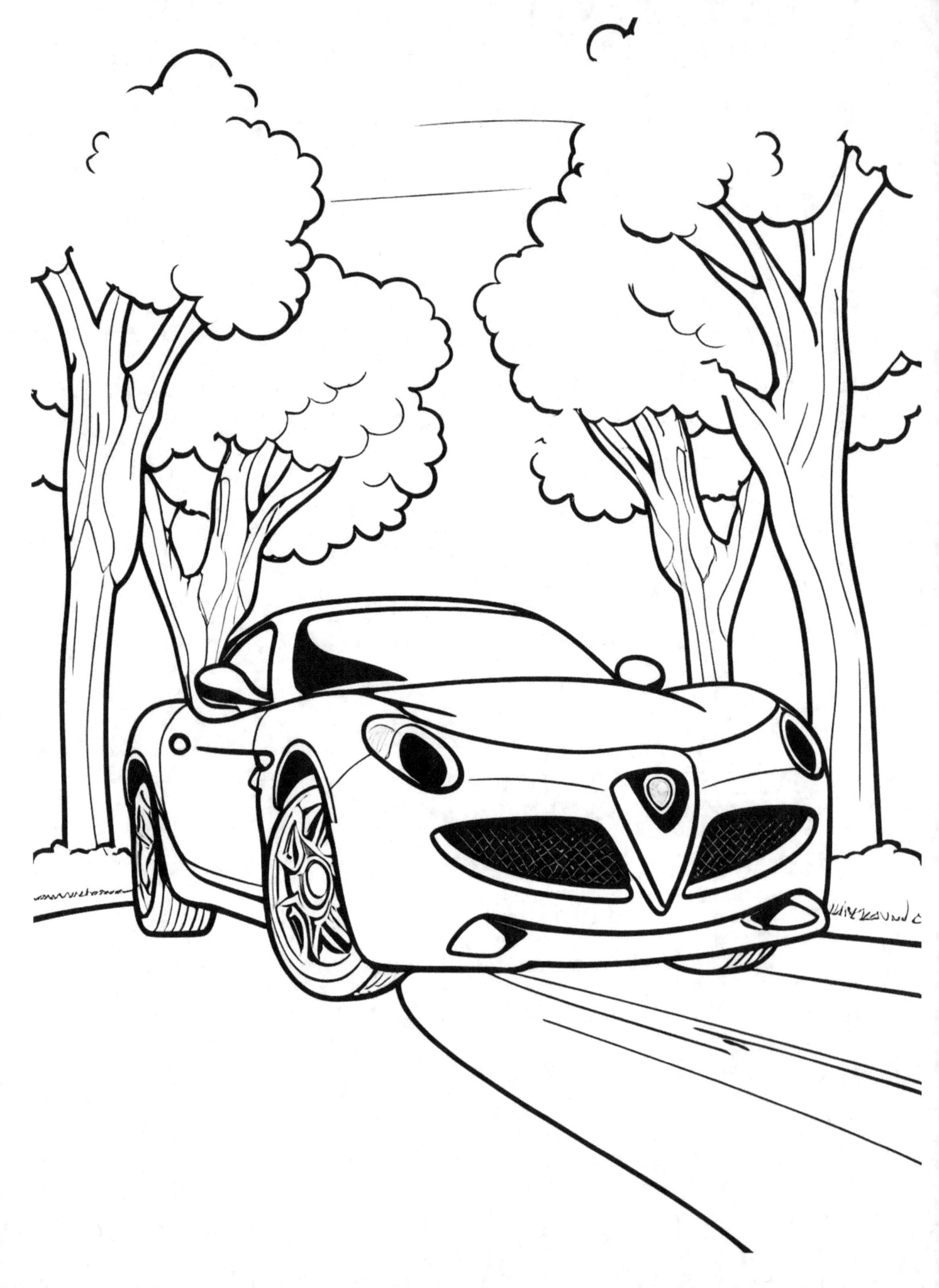

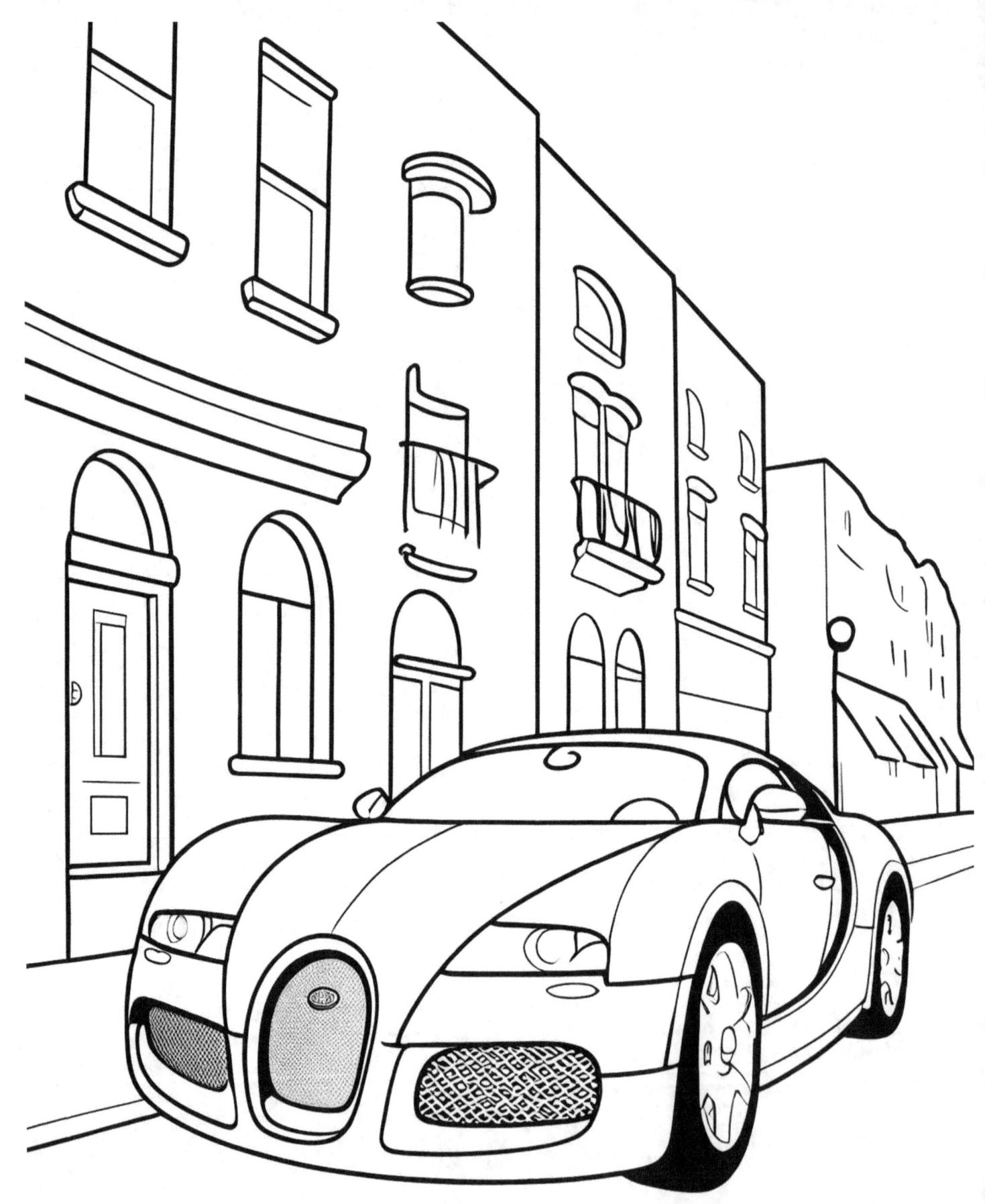

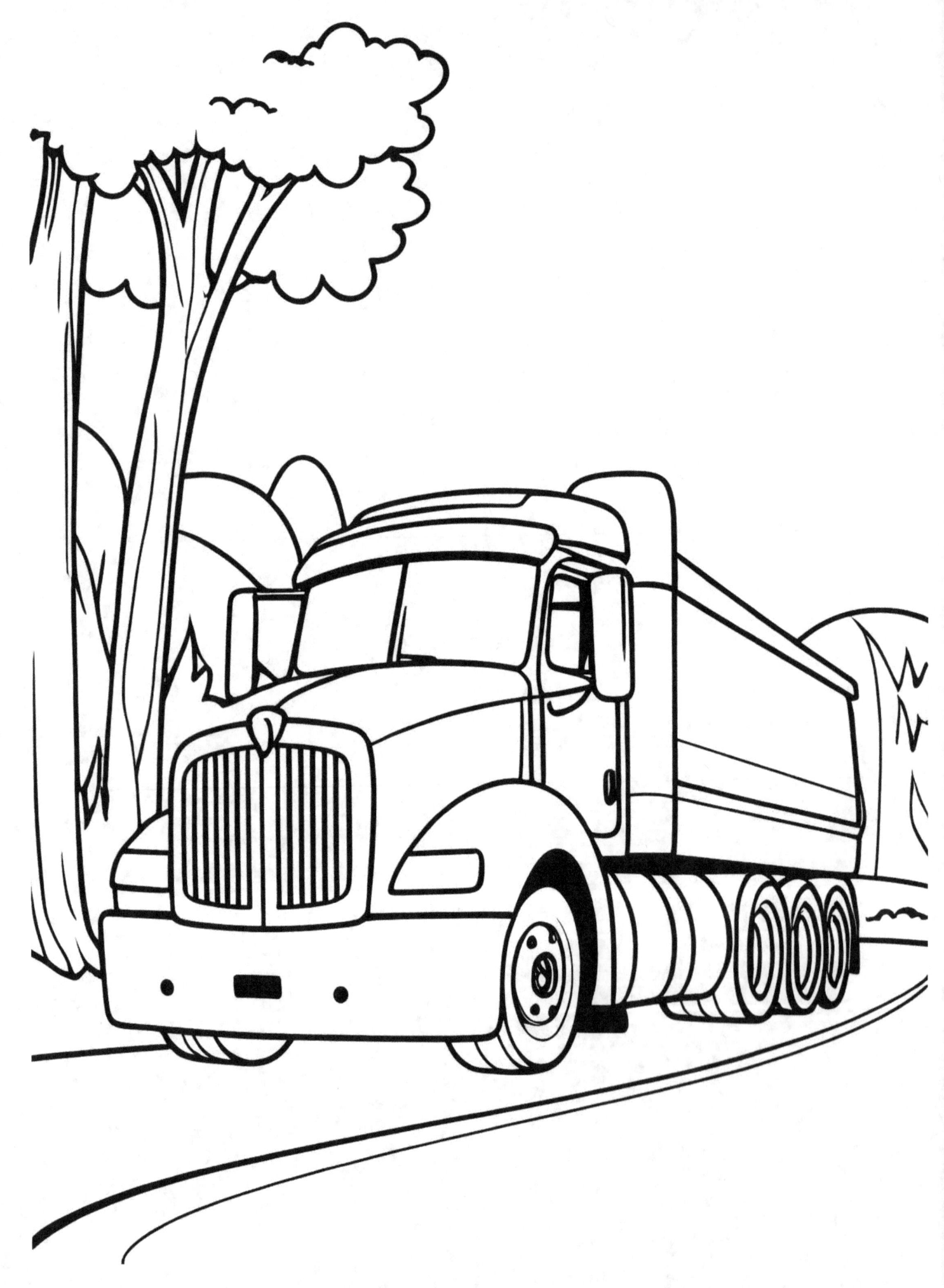

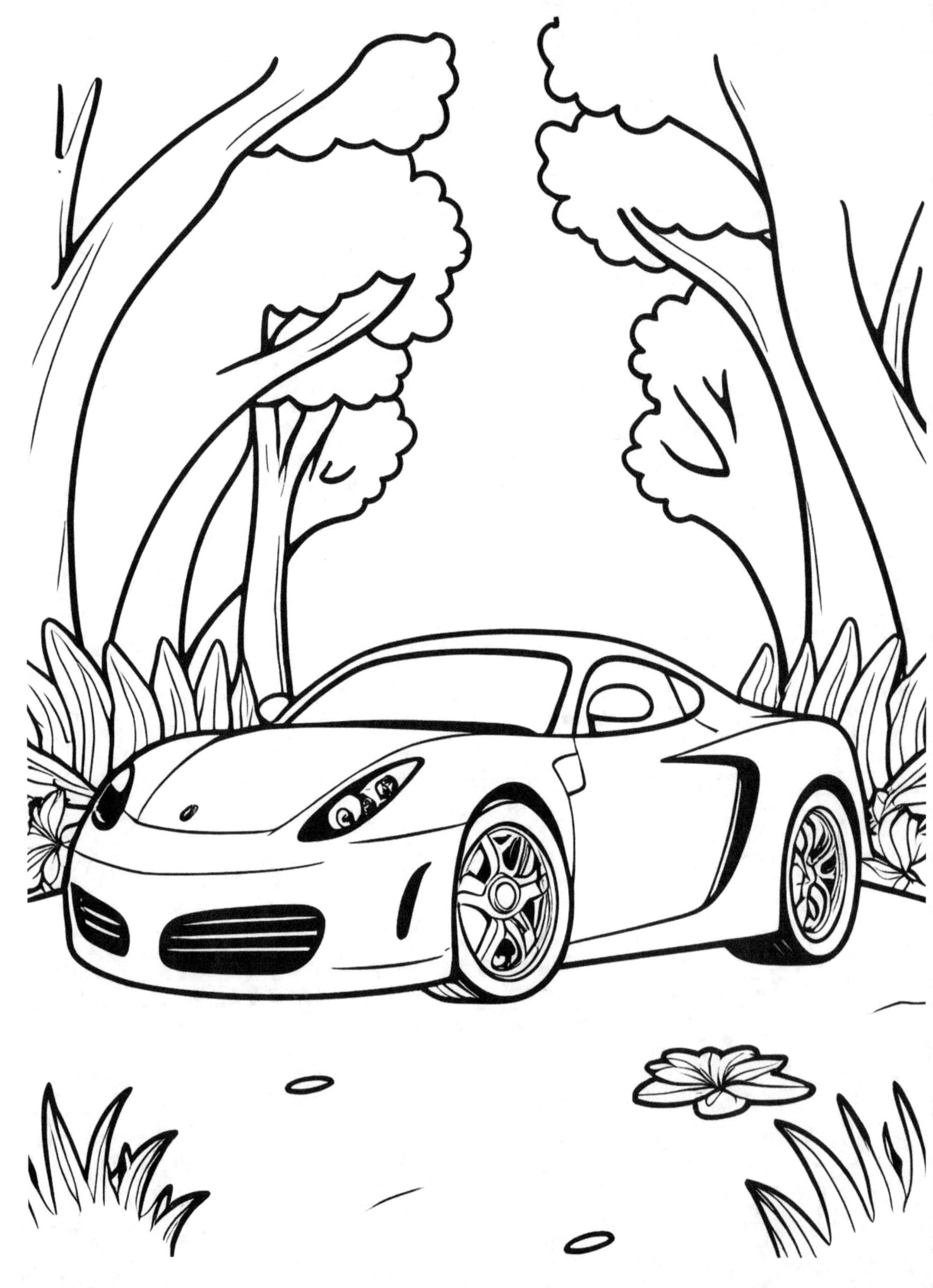

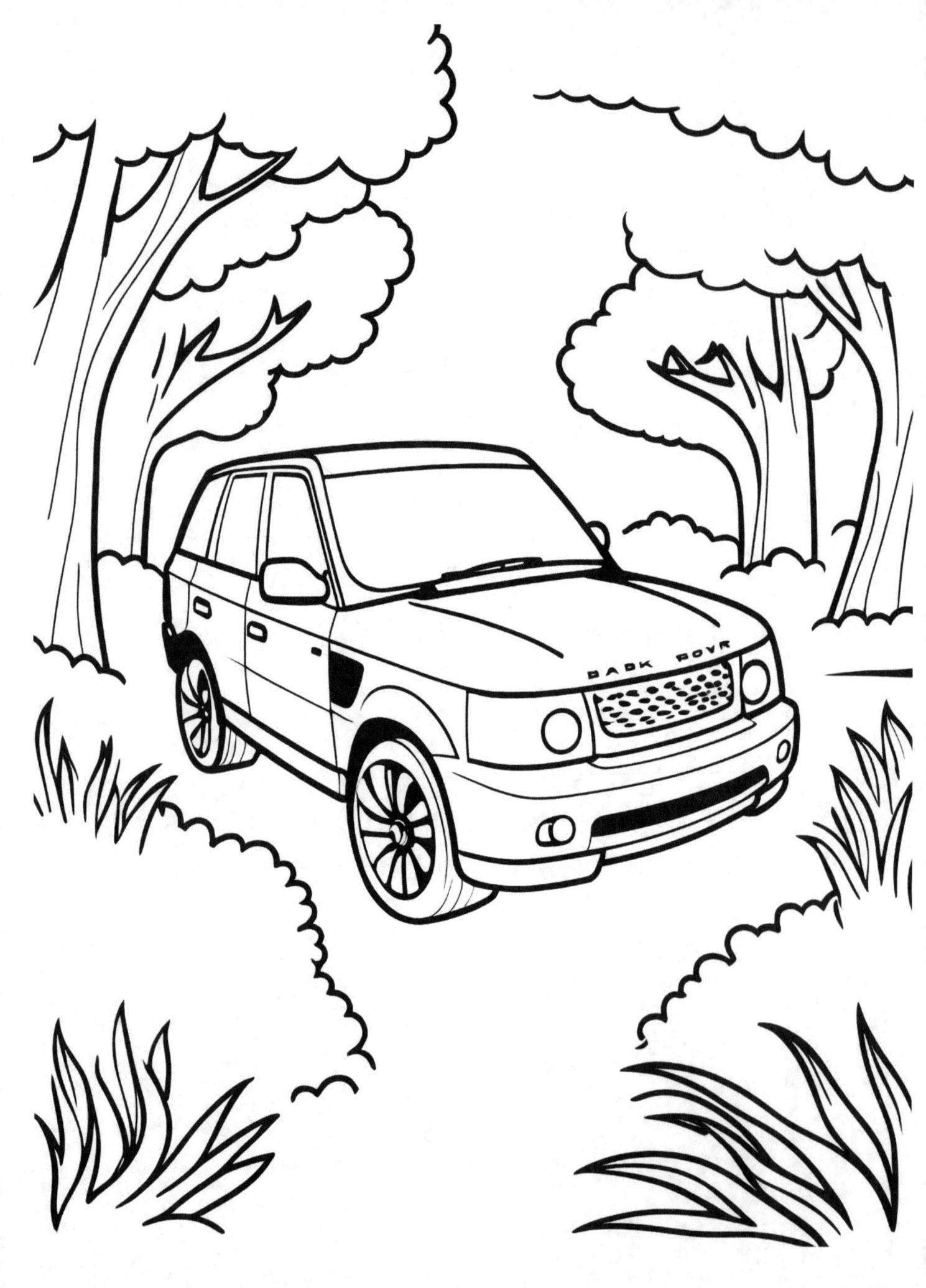

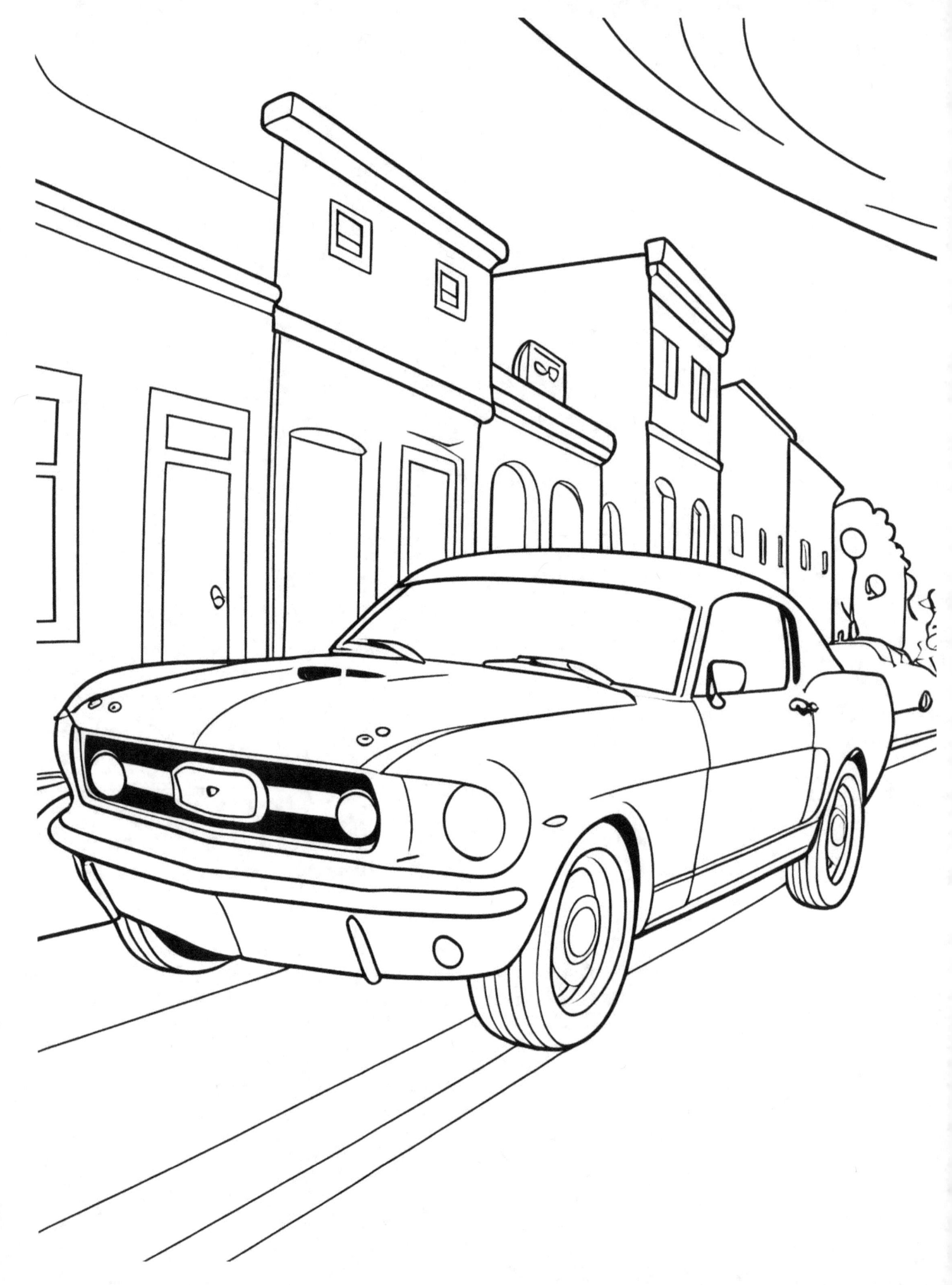

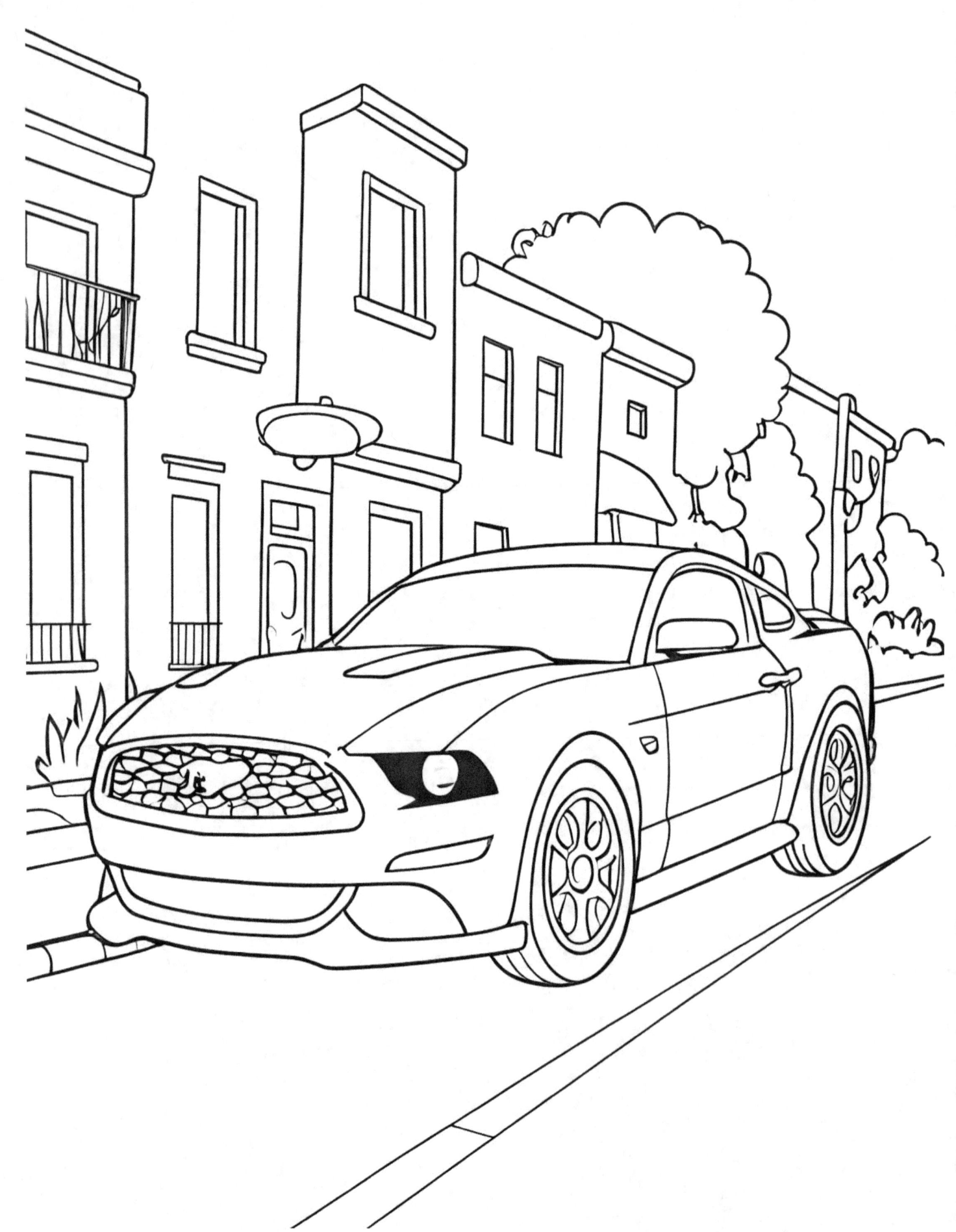

www.ingramcontent.com/pod-product-compliance
Lightning Source LLC
Chambersburg PA
CBHW082214220526
45470CB00010B/3166